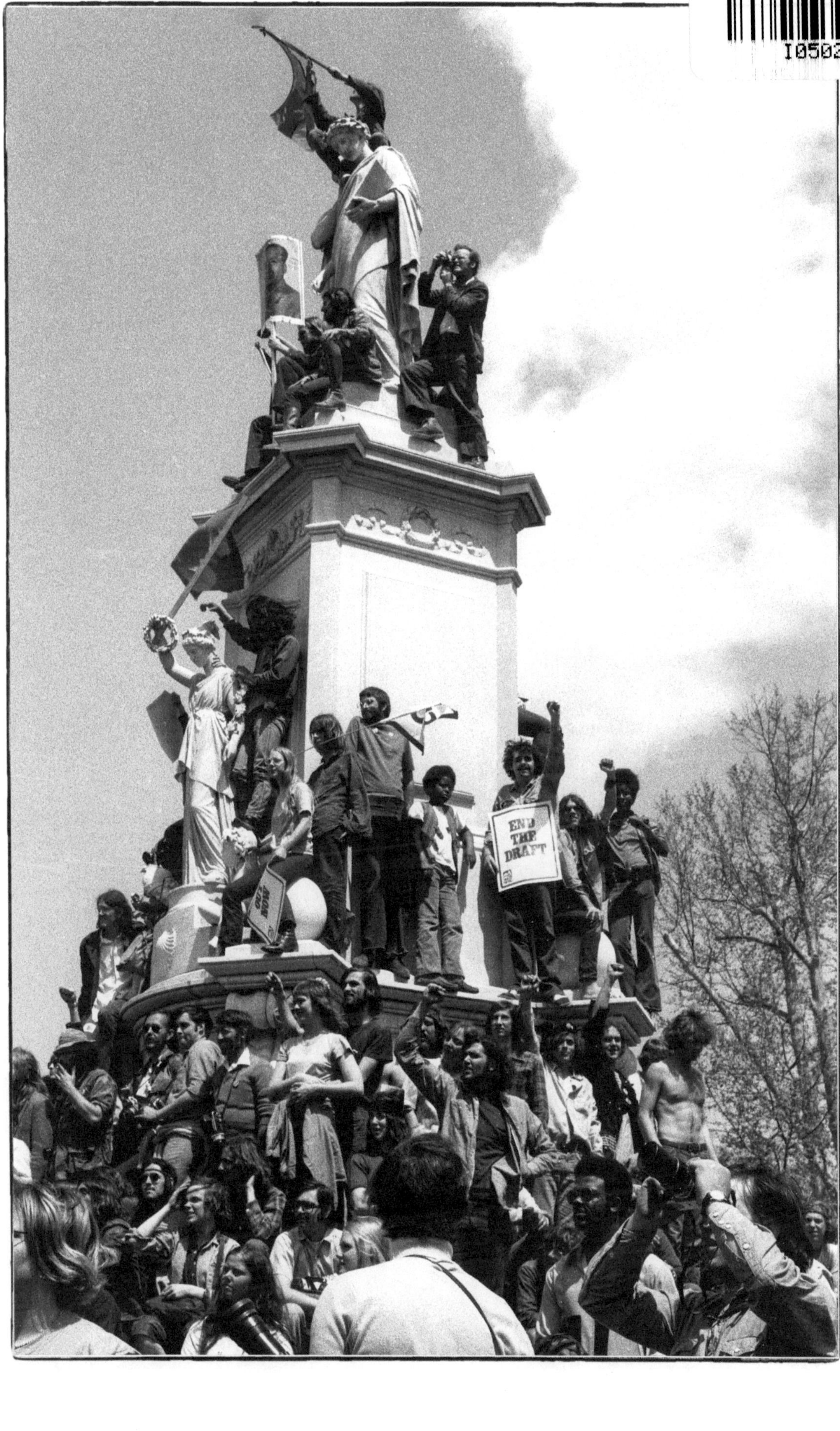
END
THE
DRAFT

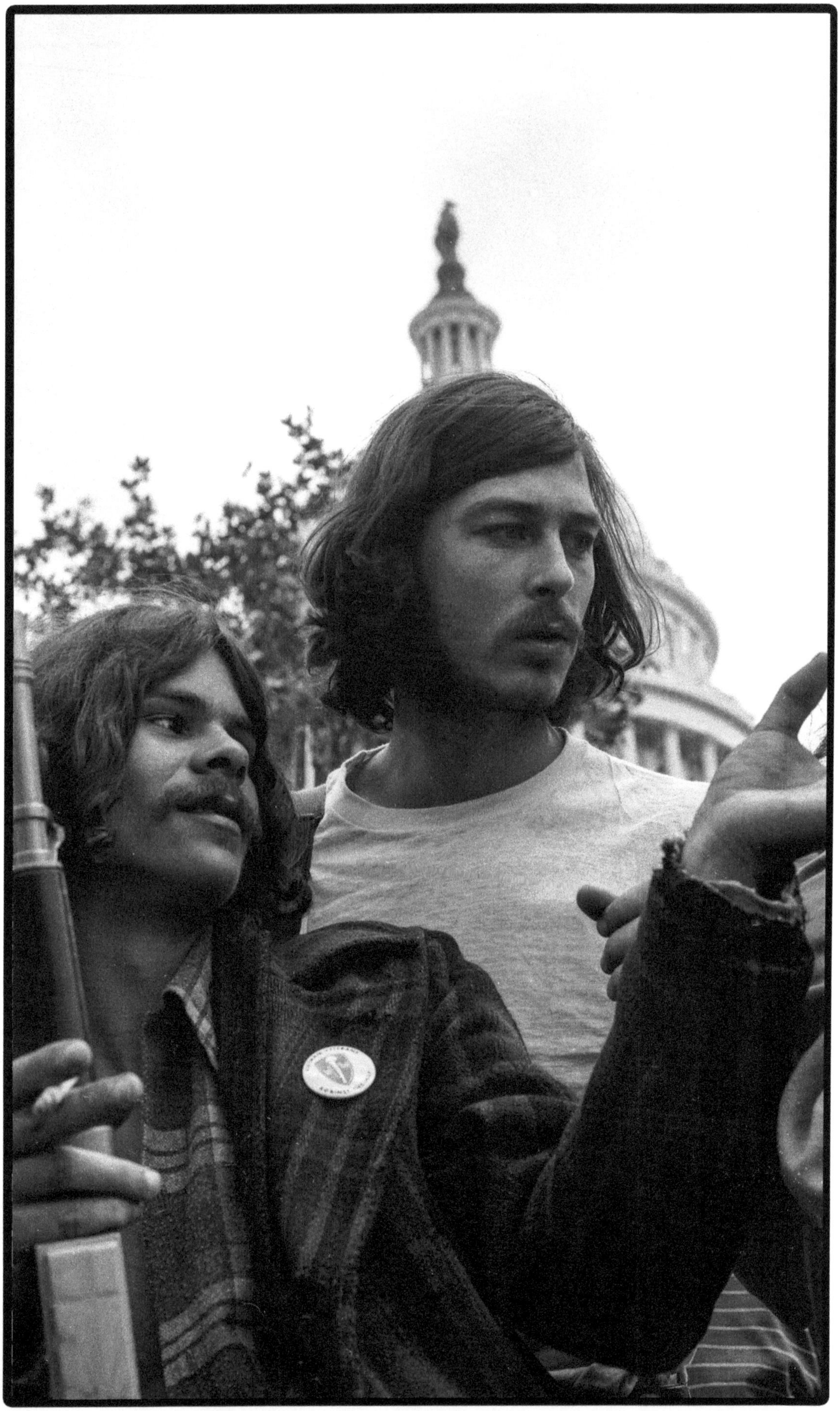

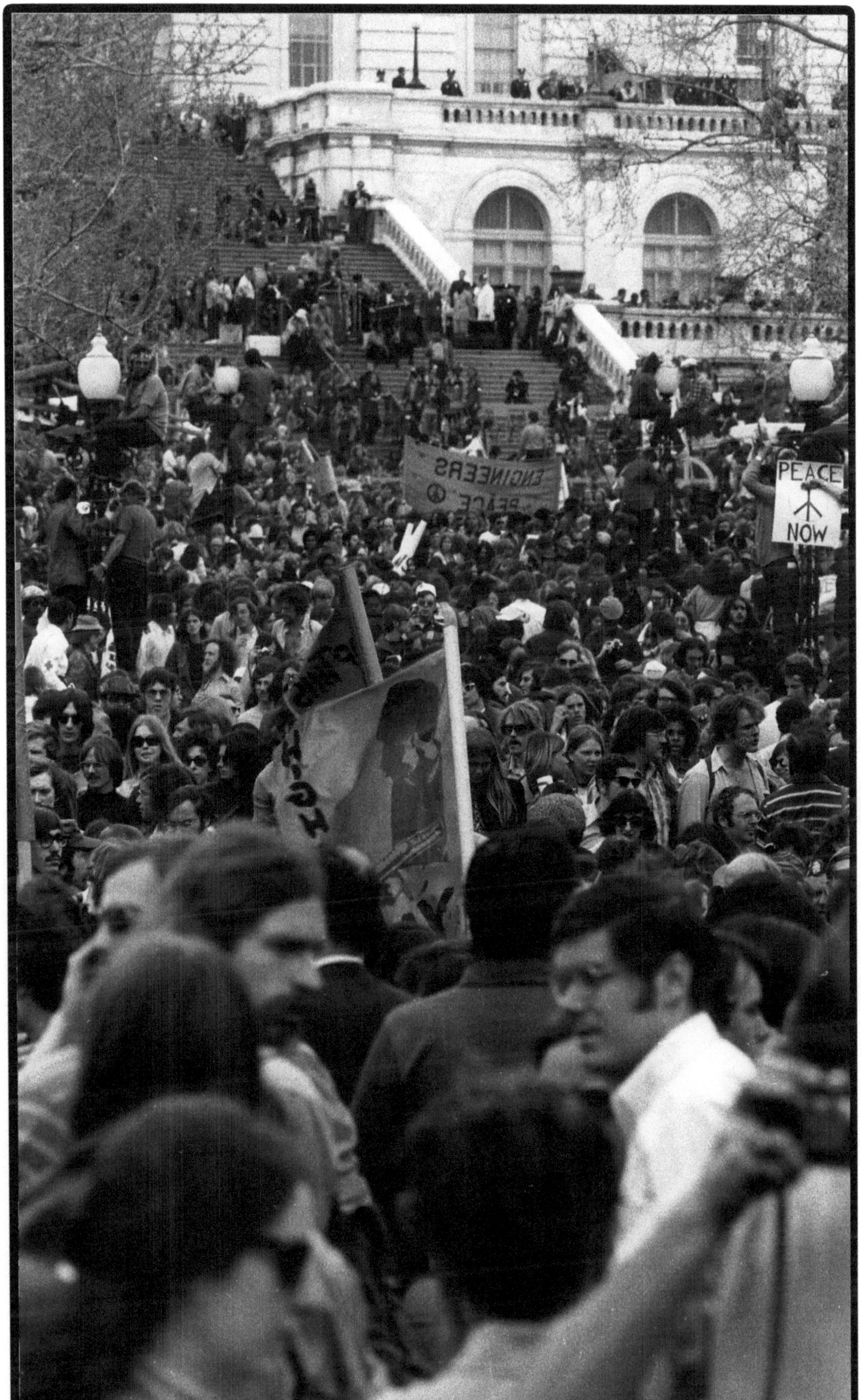
ENGINEERS
PEACE
NOW

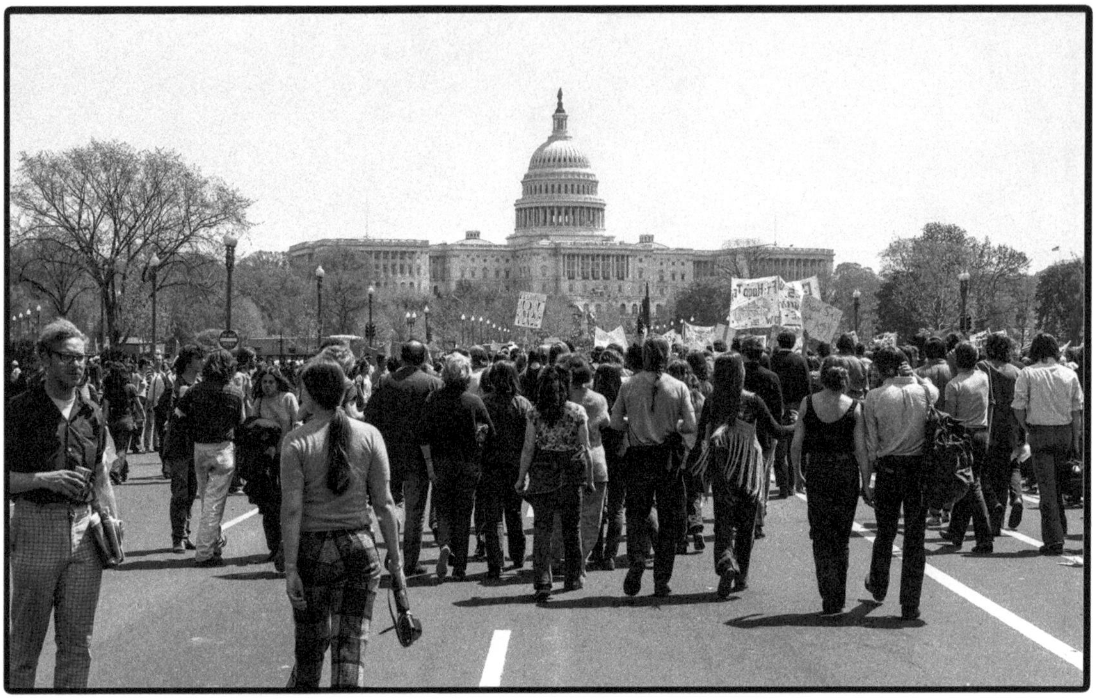

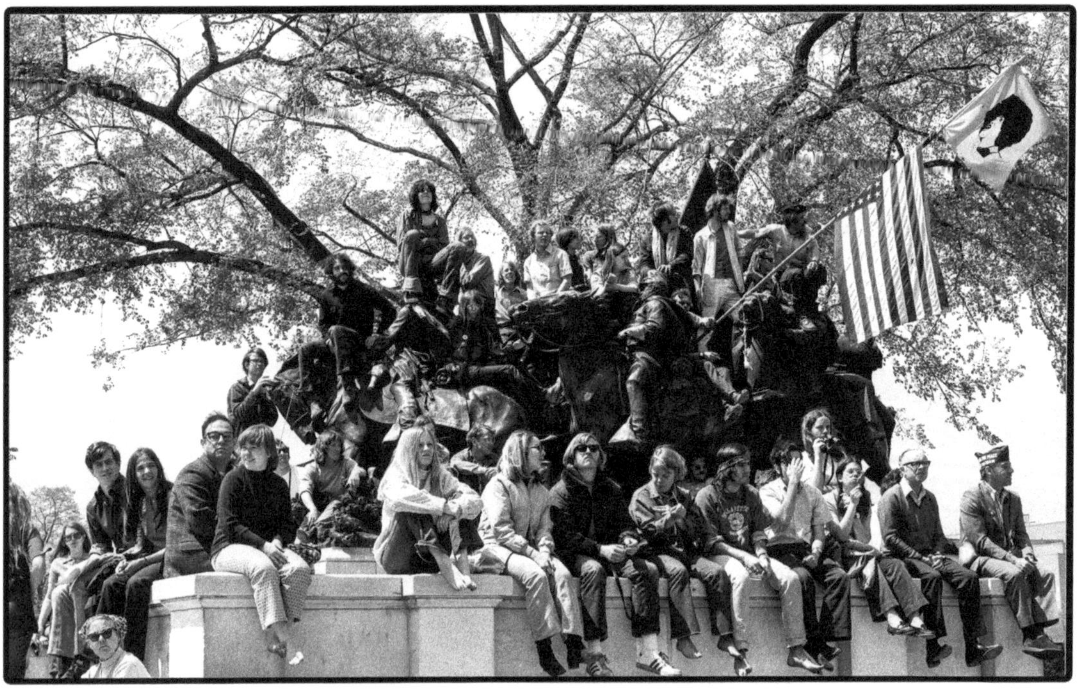

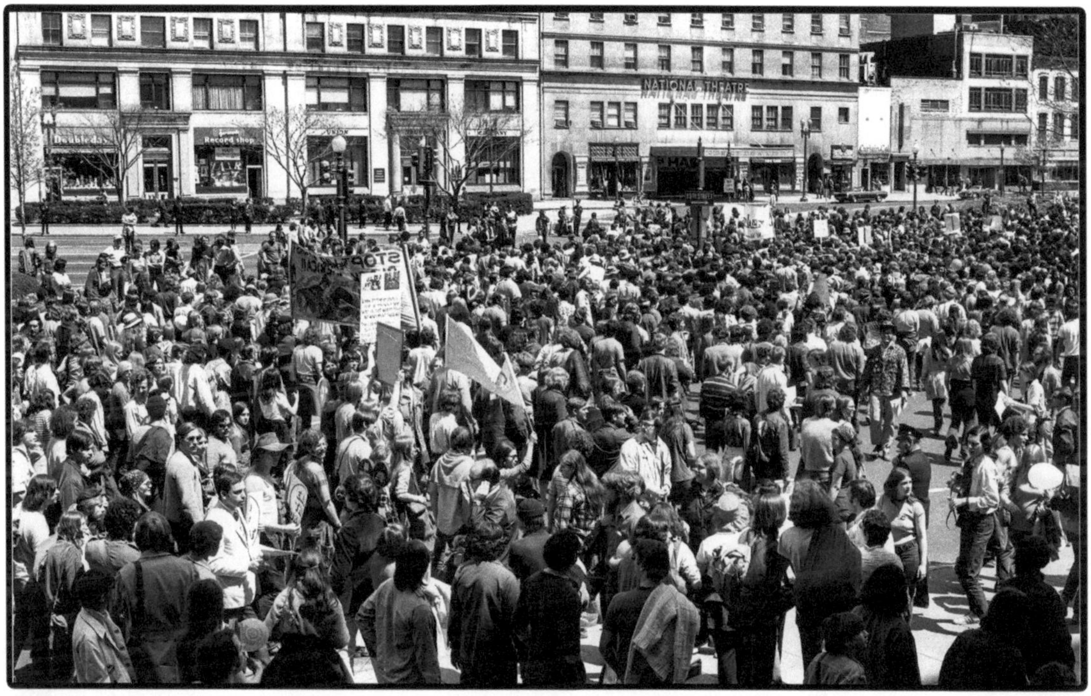
NATIONAL THEATRE

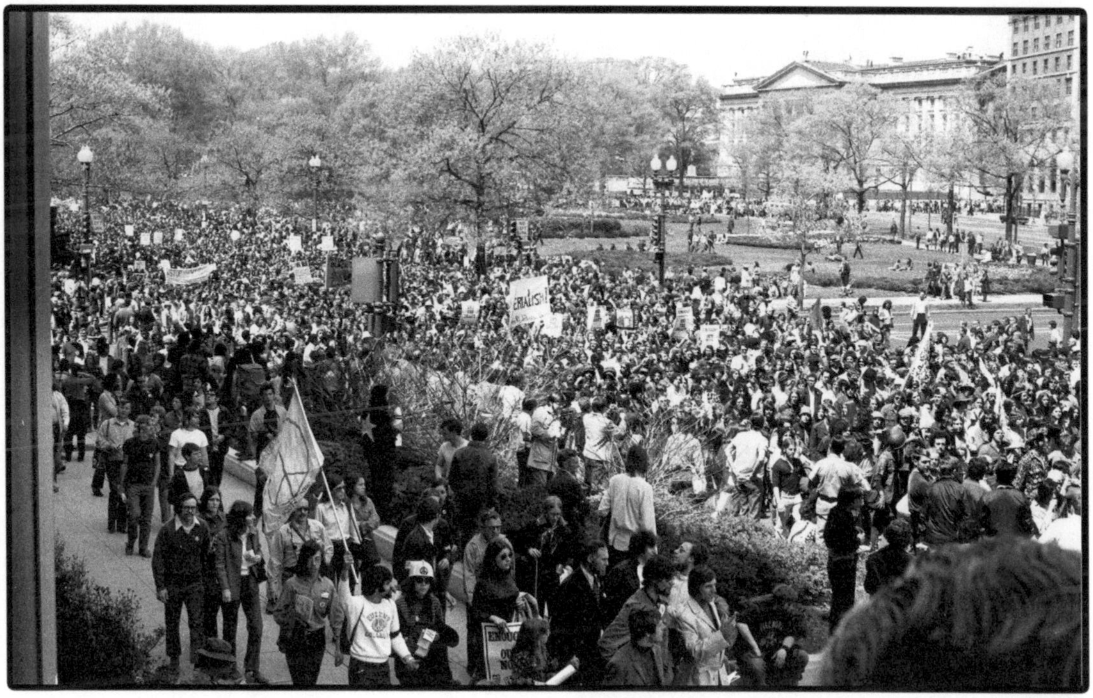

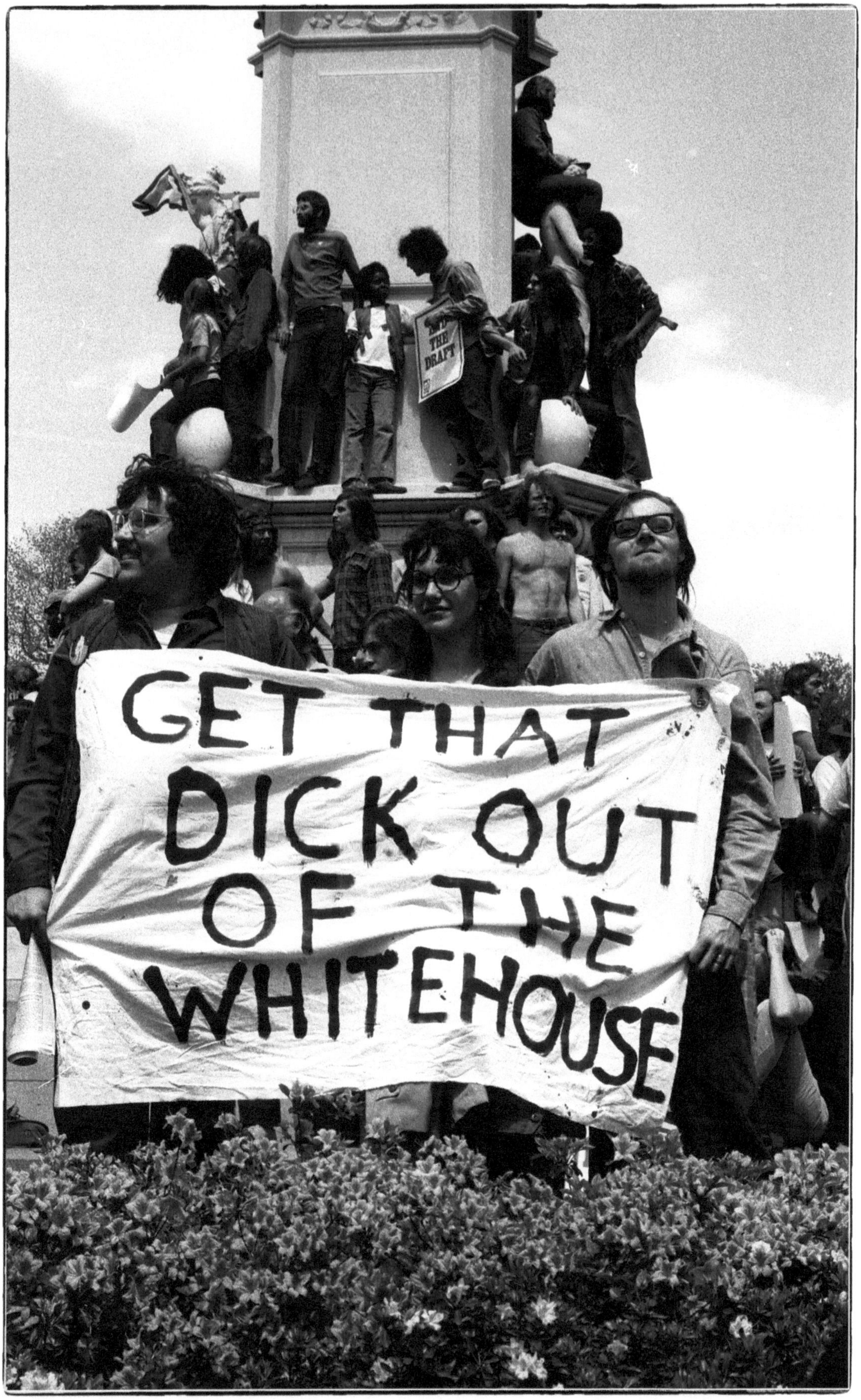
END THE DRAFT
GET THAT DICK OUT OF THE WHITEHOUSE

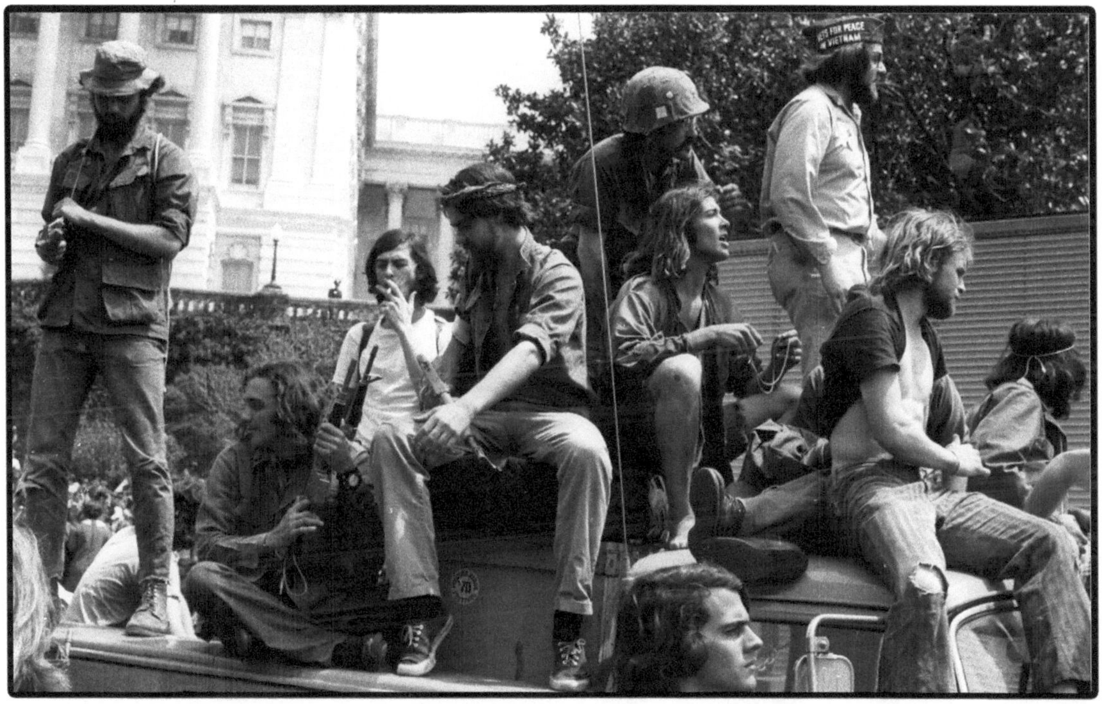

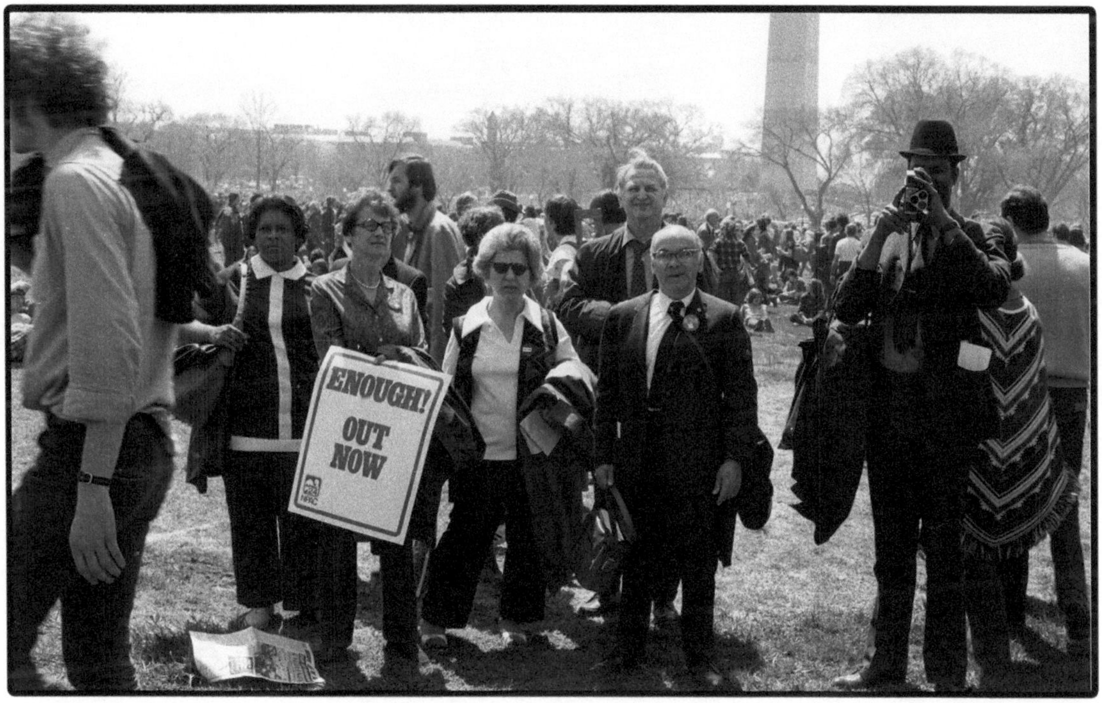
ENOUGH!
OUT
NOW

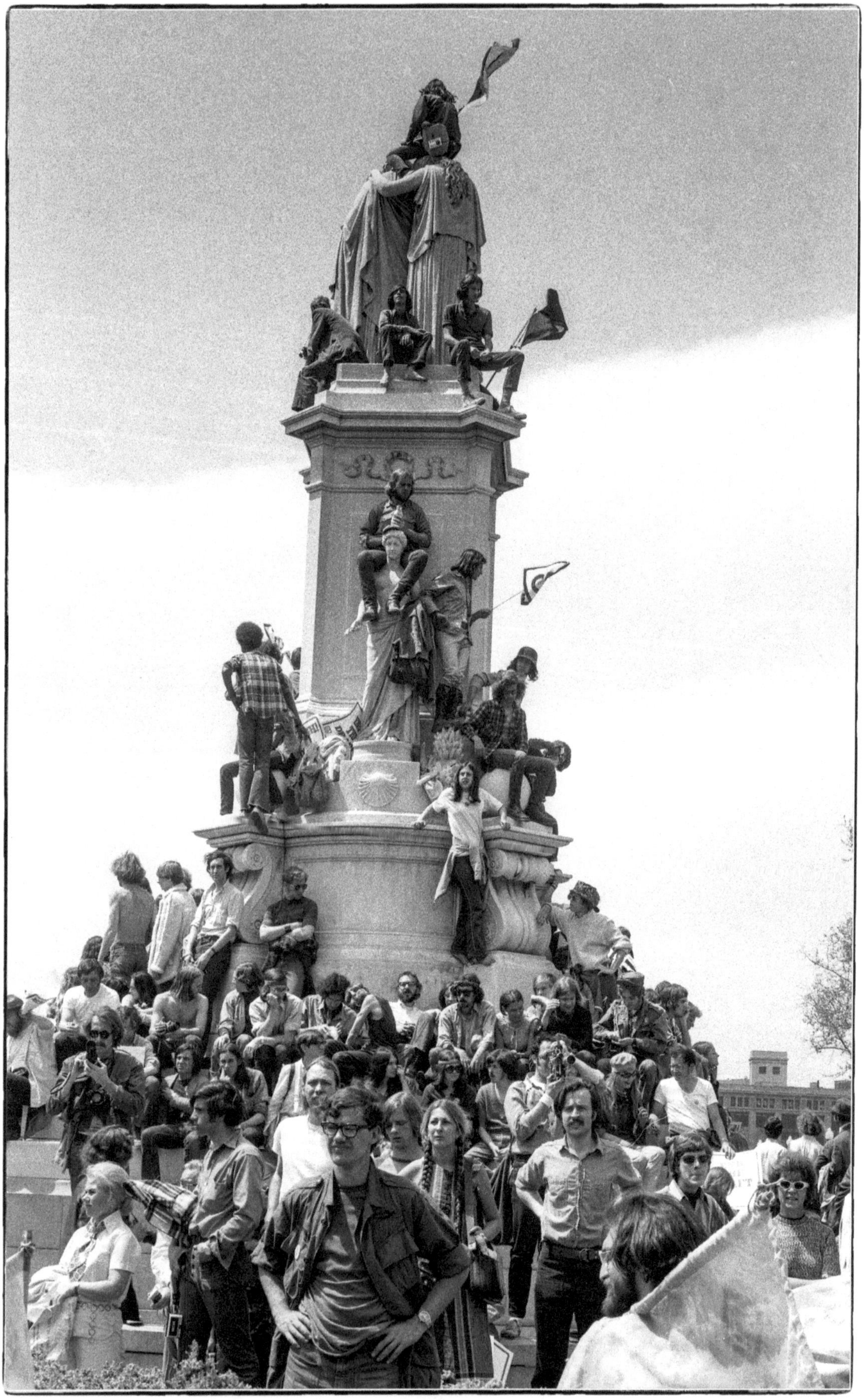

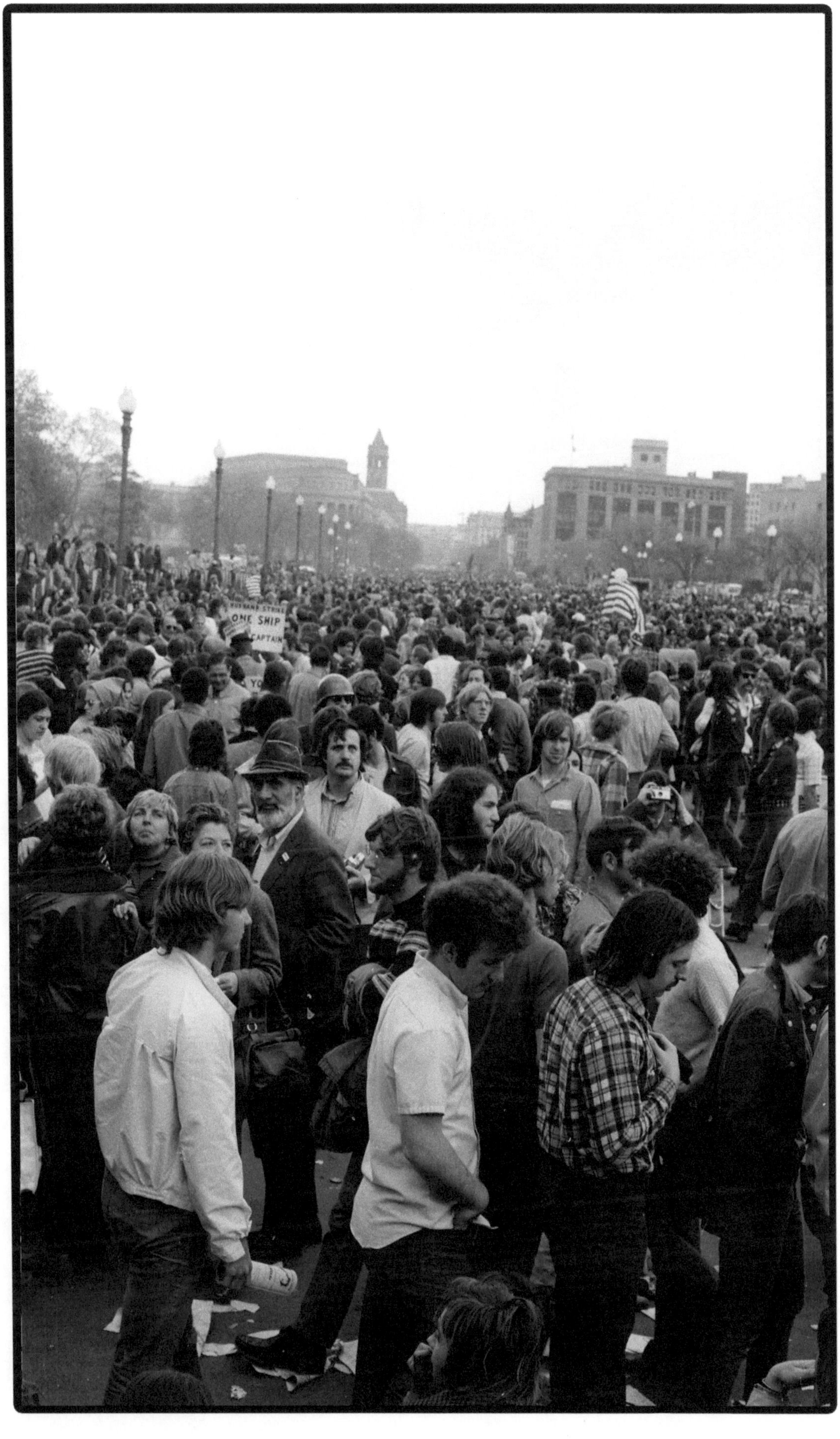
ONE SHIP
CAPTAIN

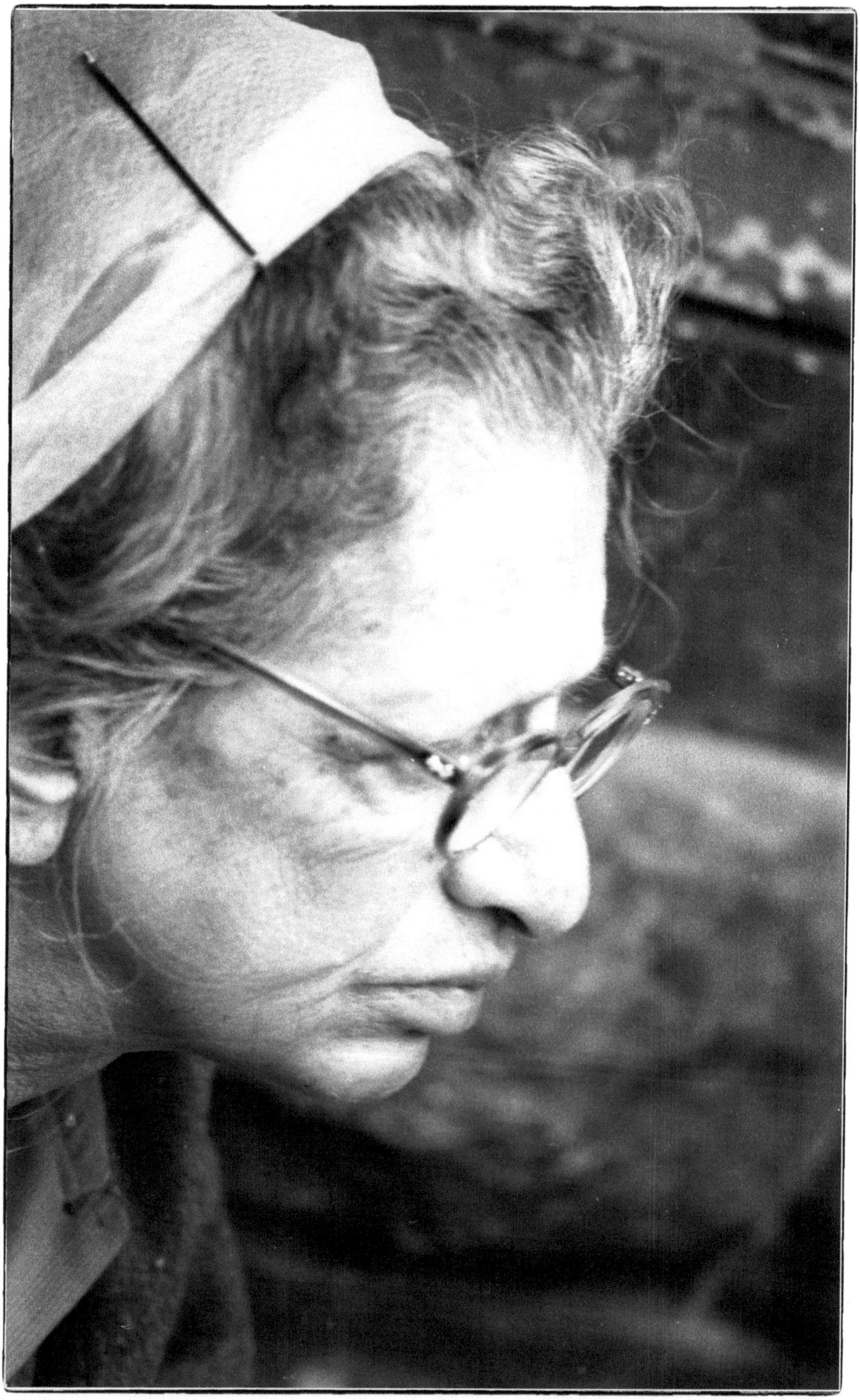

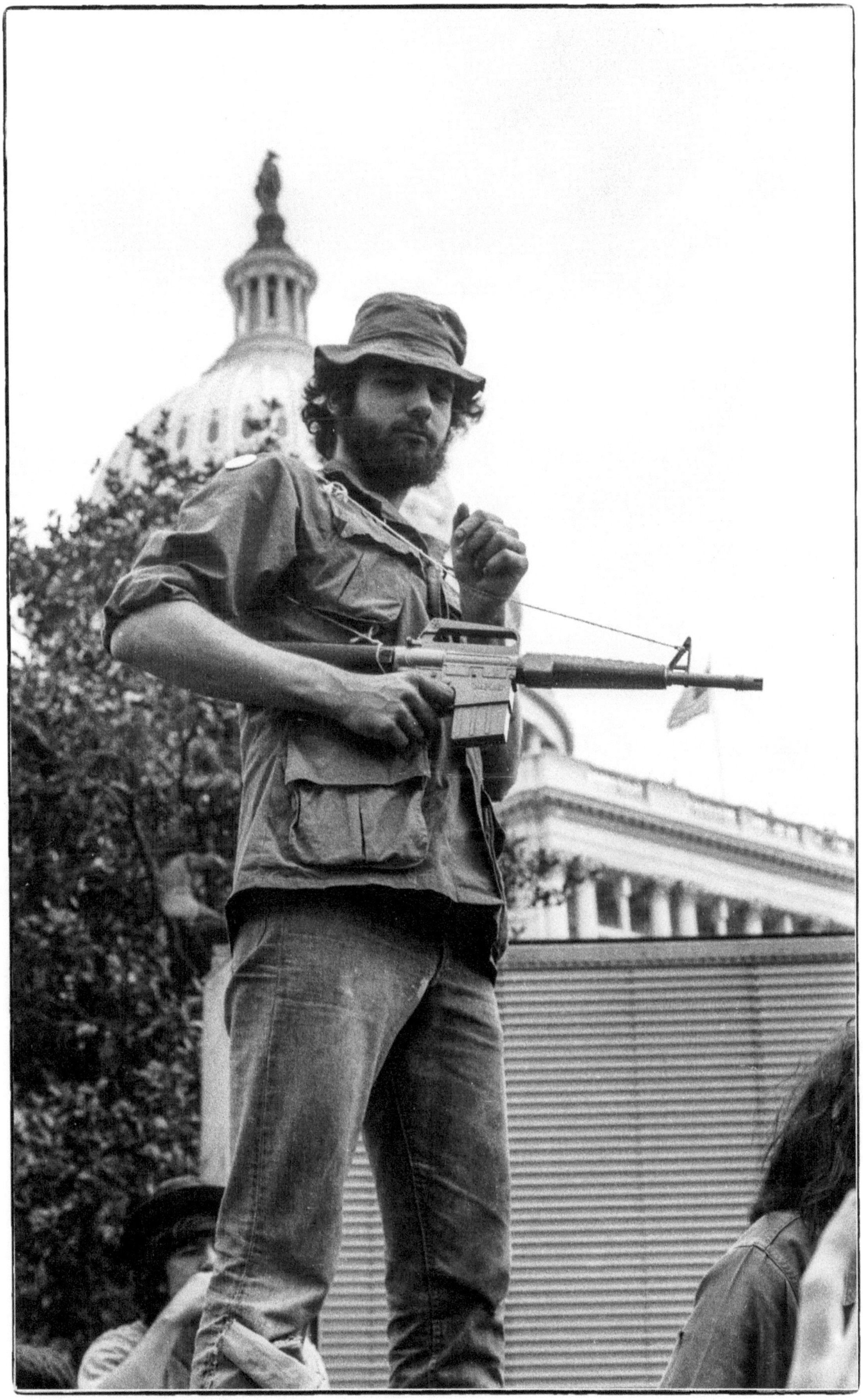

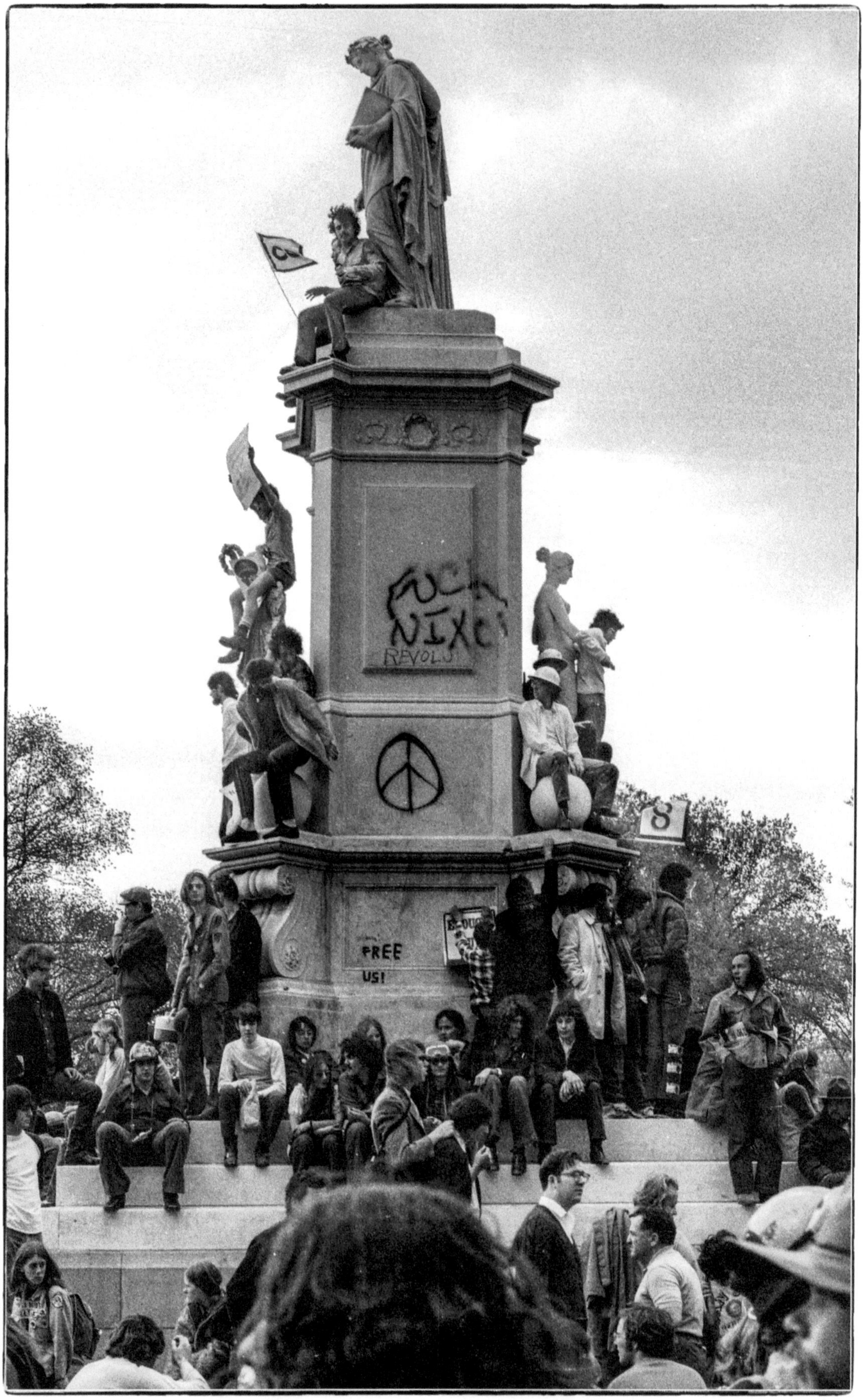
REVOLU
FREE
US!
8

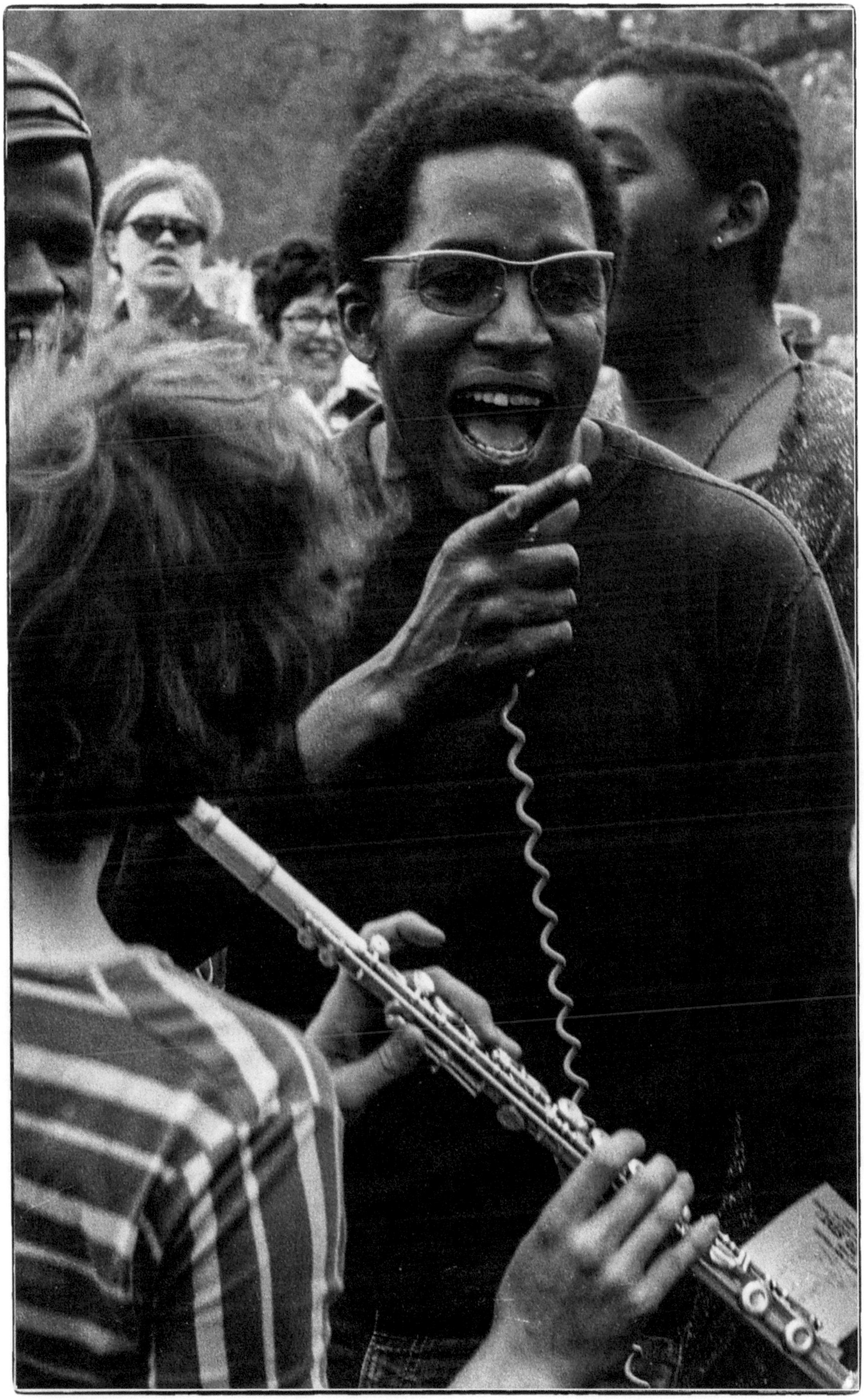

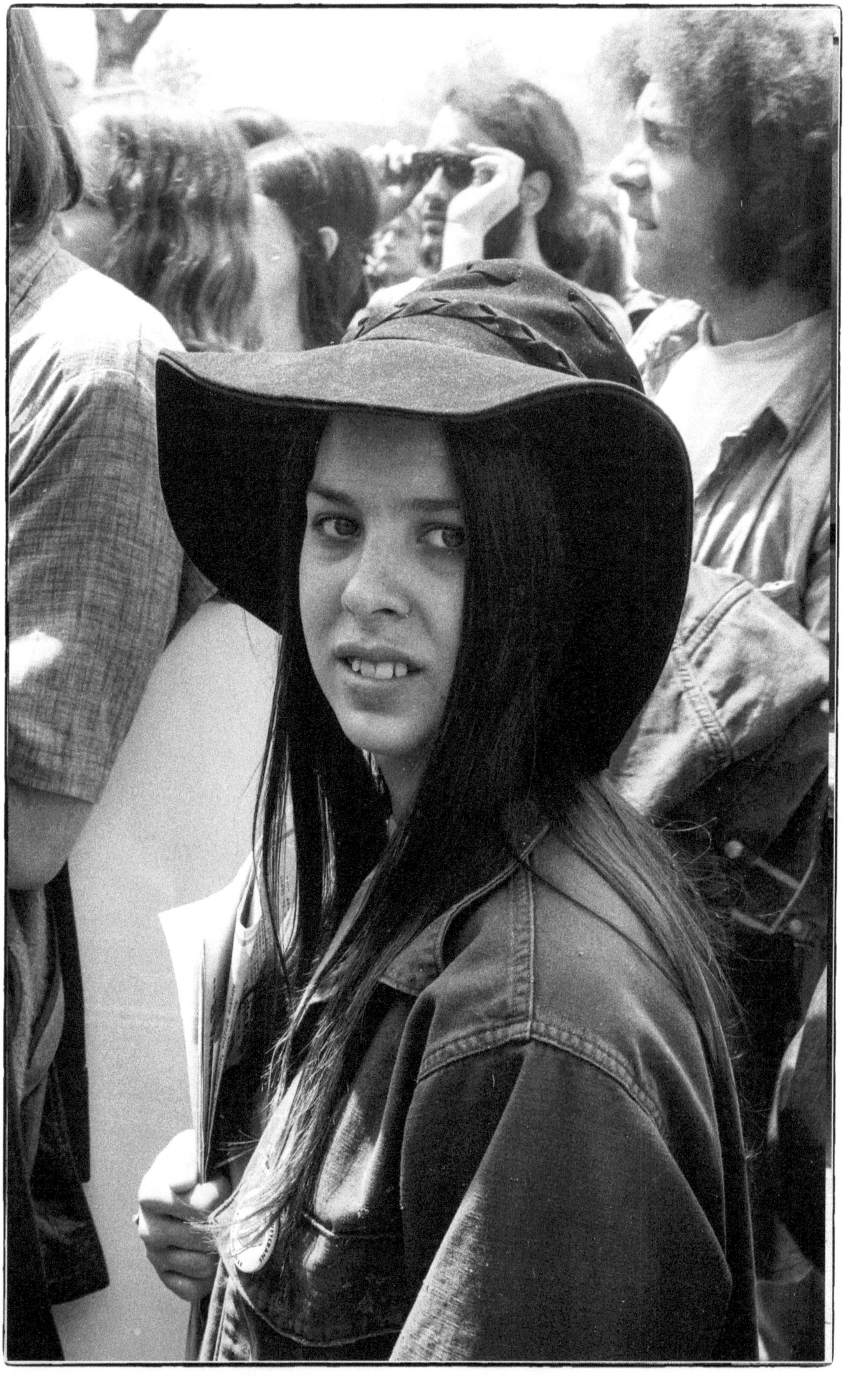

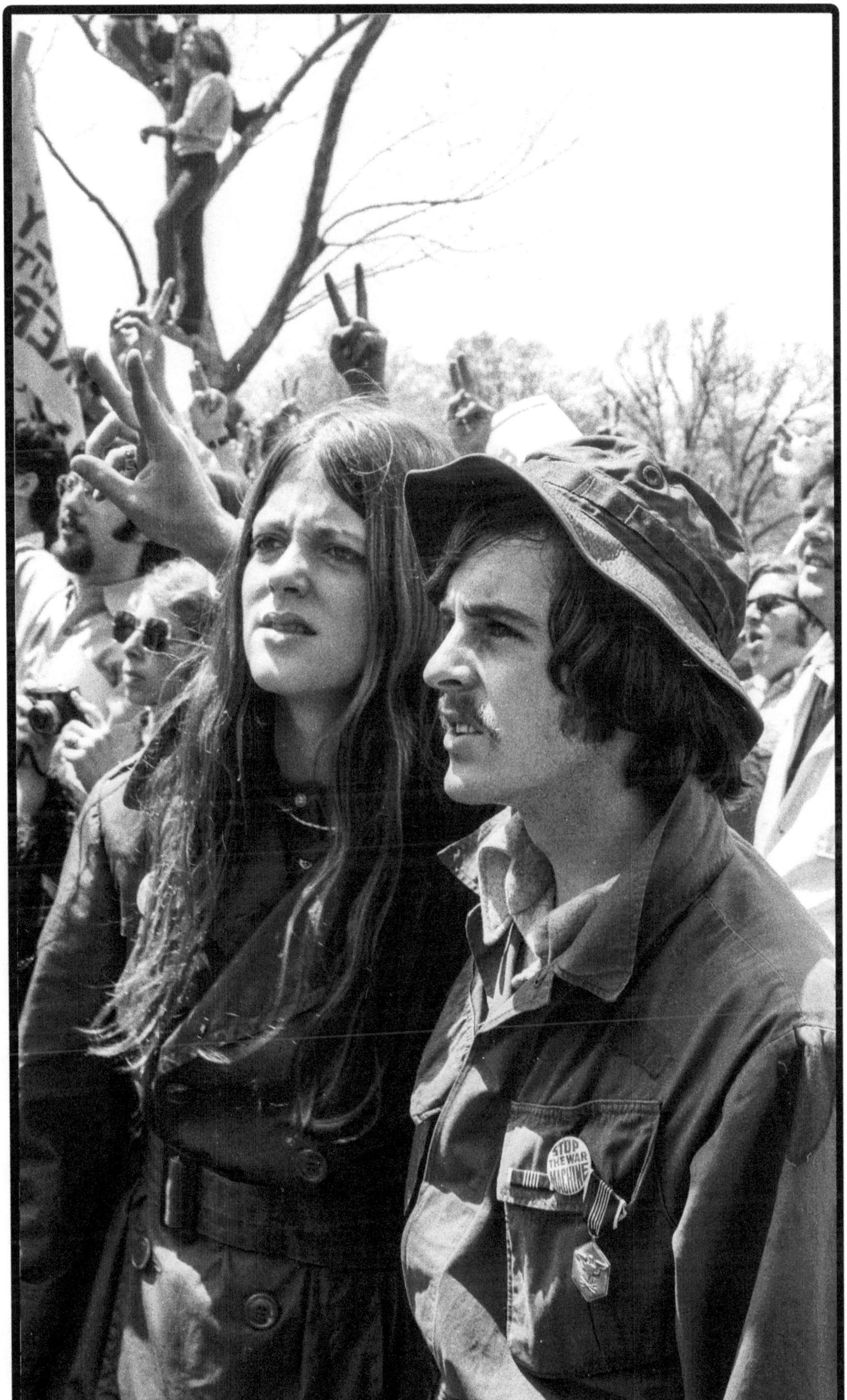
STOP THE WAR MACHINE

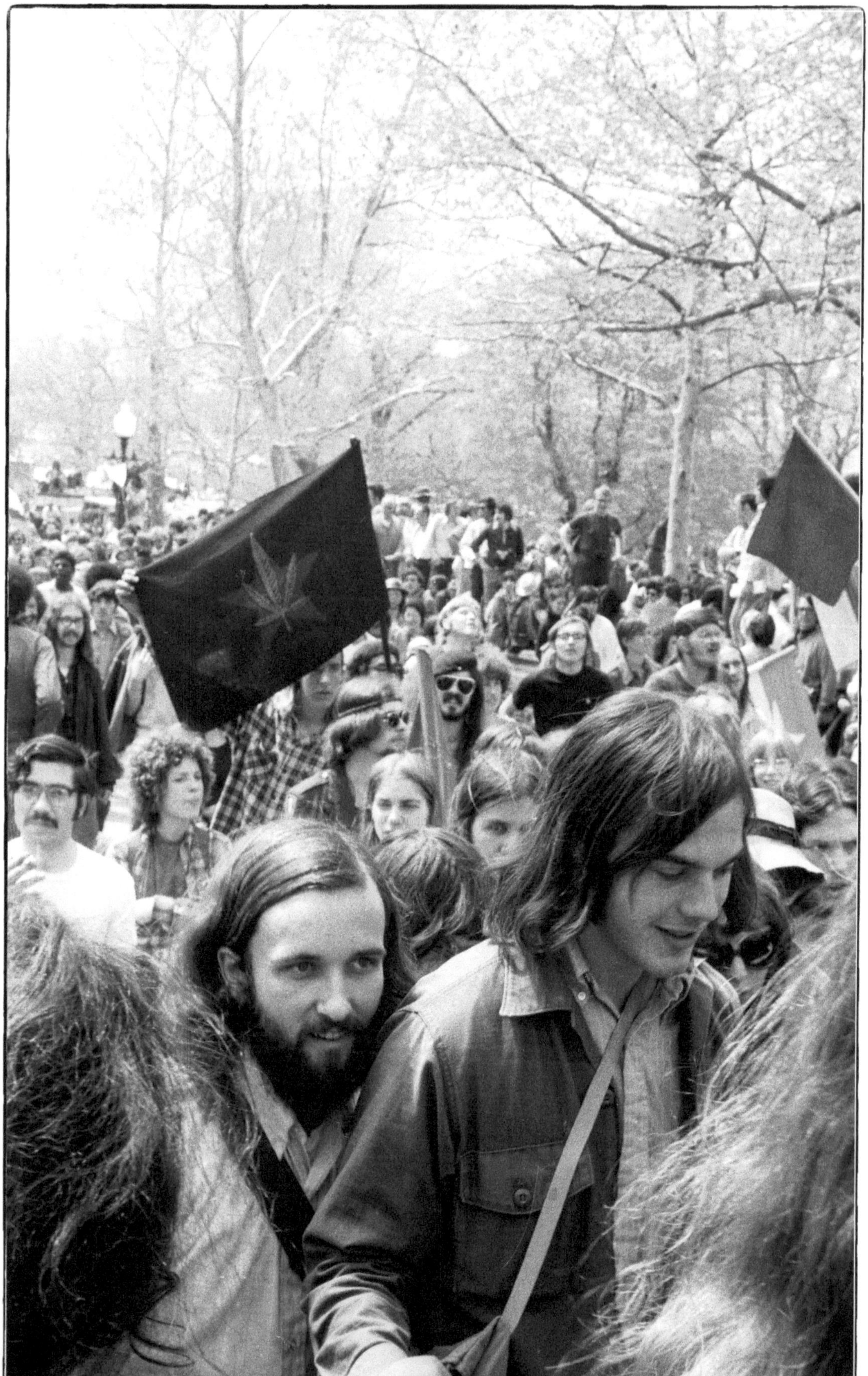

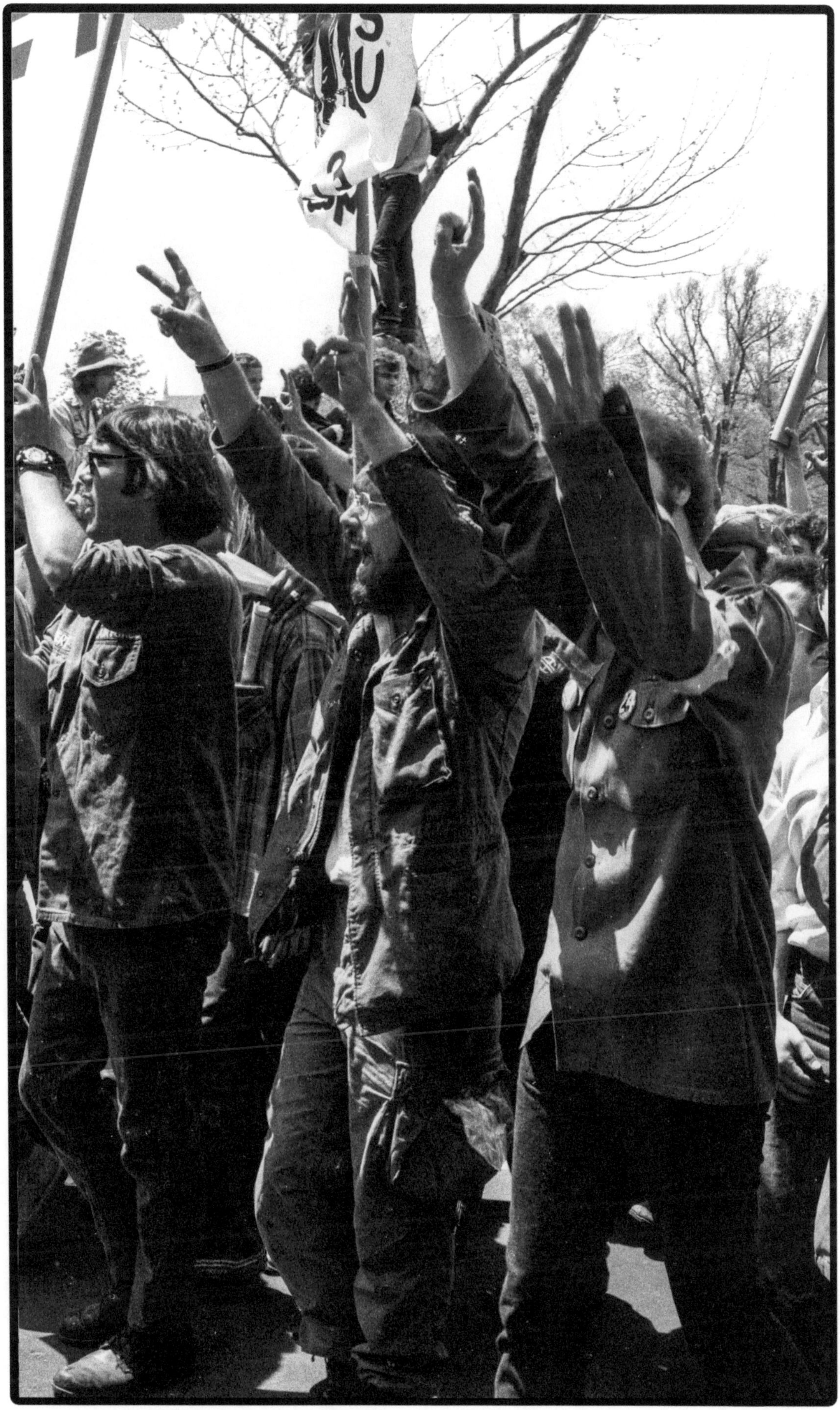

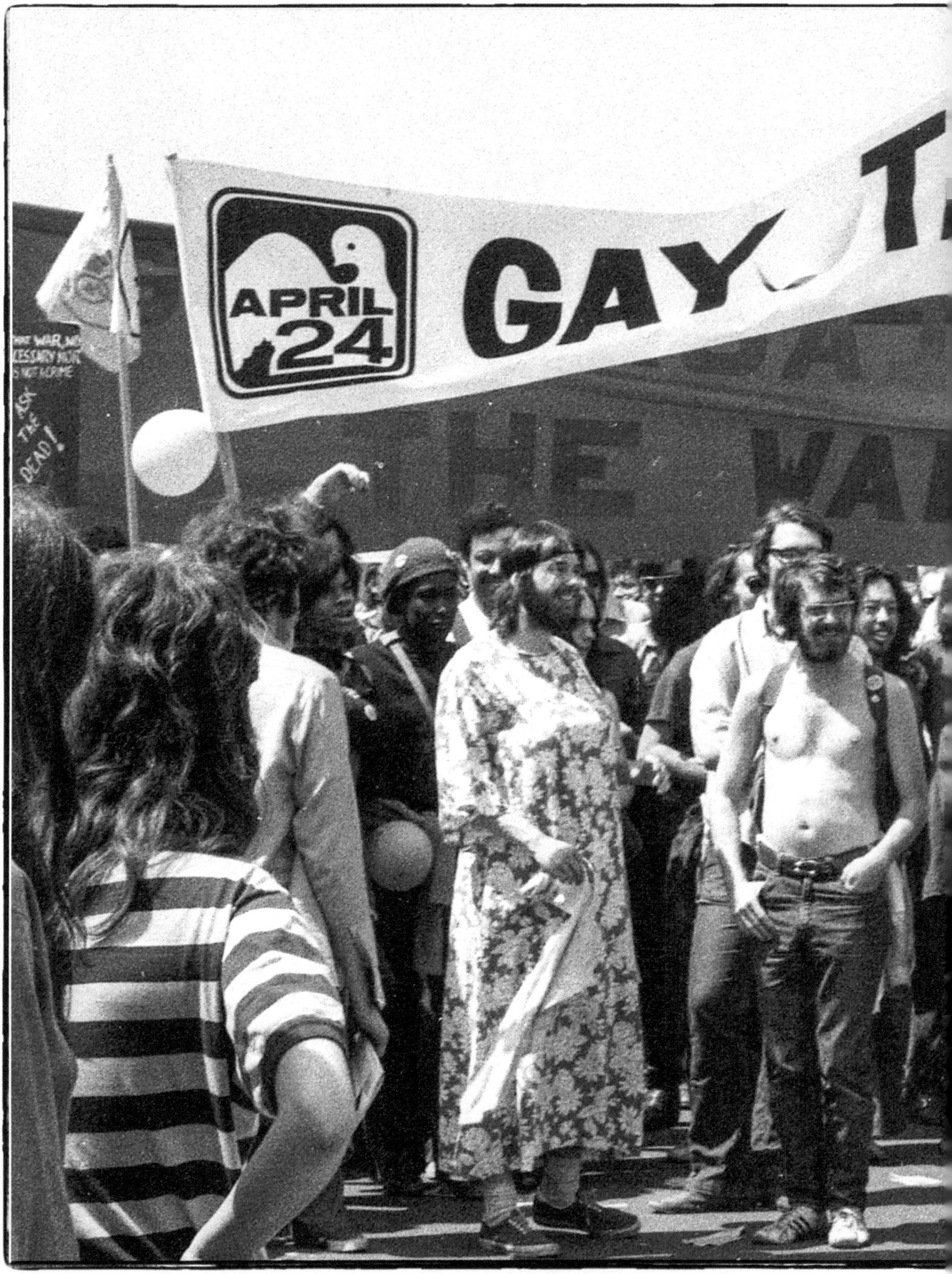
APRIL
24
GAY
ASK THE DEAD!

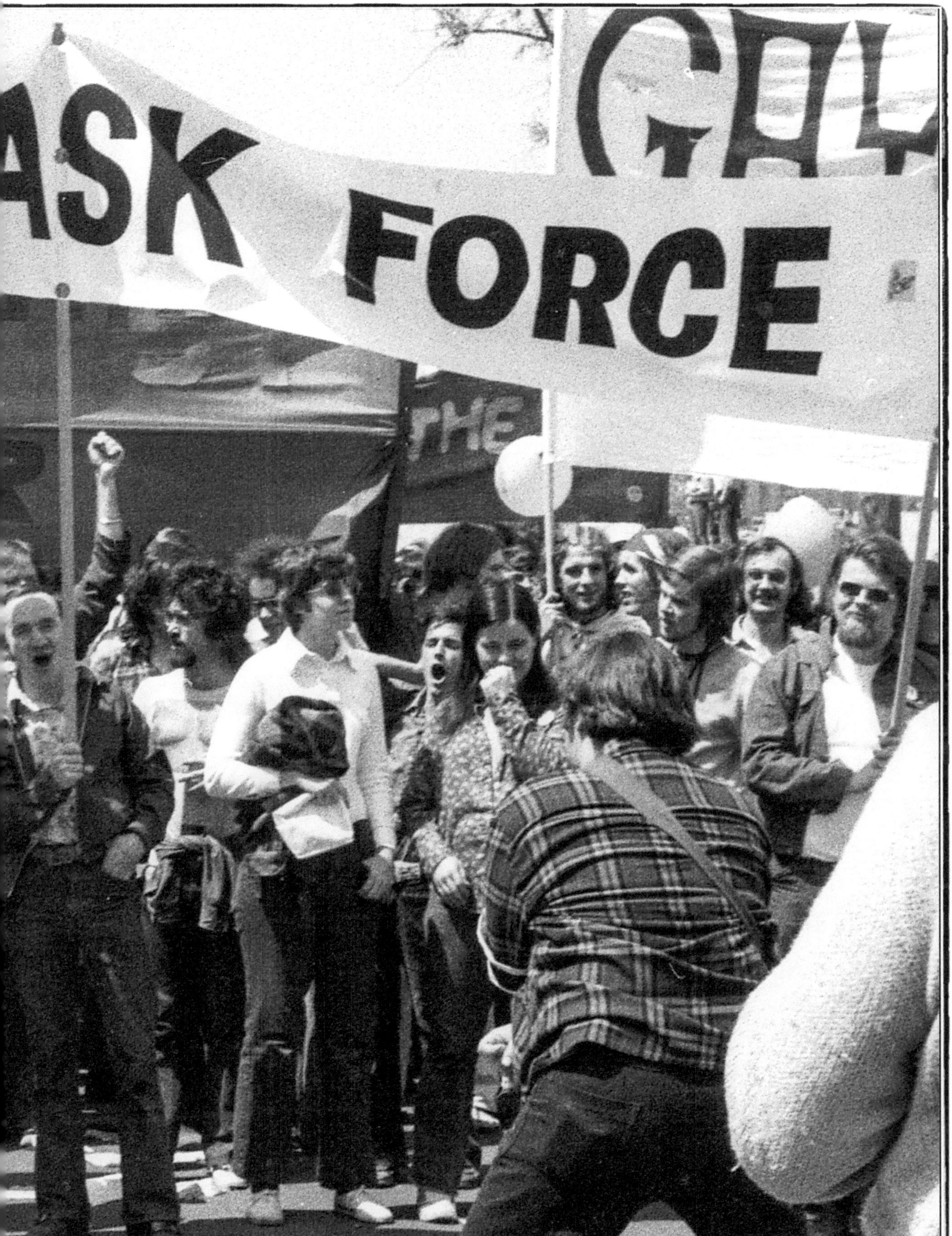
ASK FORCE
THE

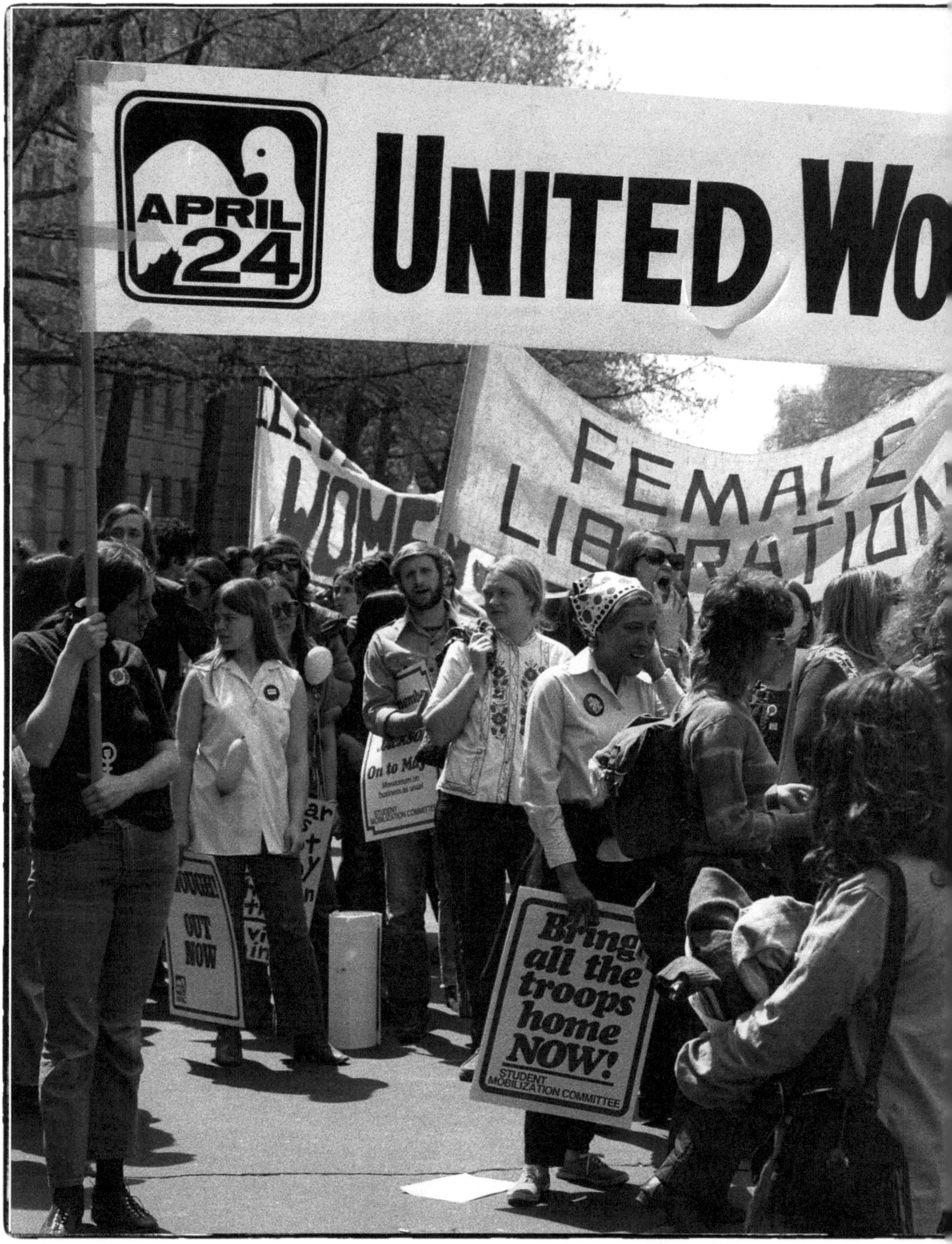

APRIL 24
UNITED WO
FEMALE
LIBERATION
OUT NOW
On to May
STUDENT MOBILIZATION COMMITTEE
Bring all the troops home NOW!
STUDENT MOBILIZATION COMMITTEE

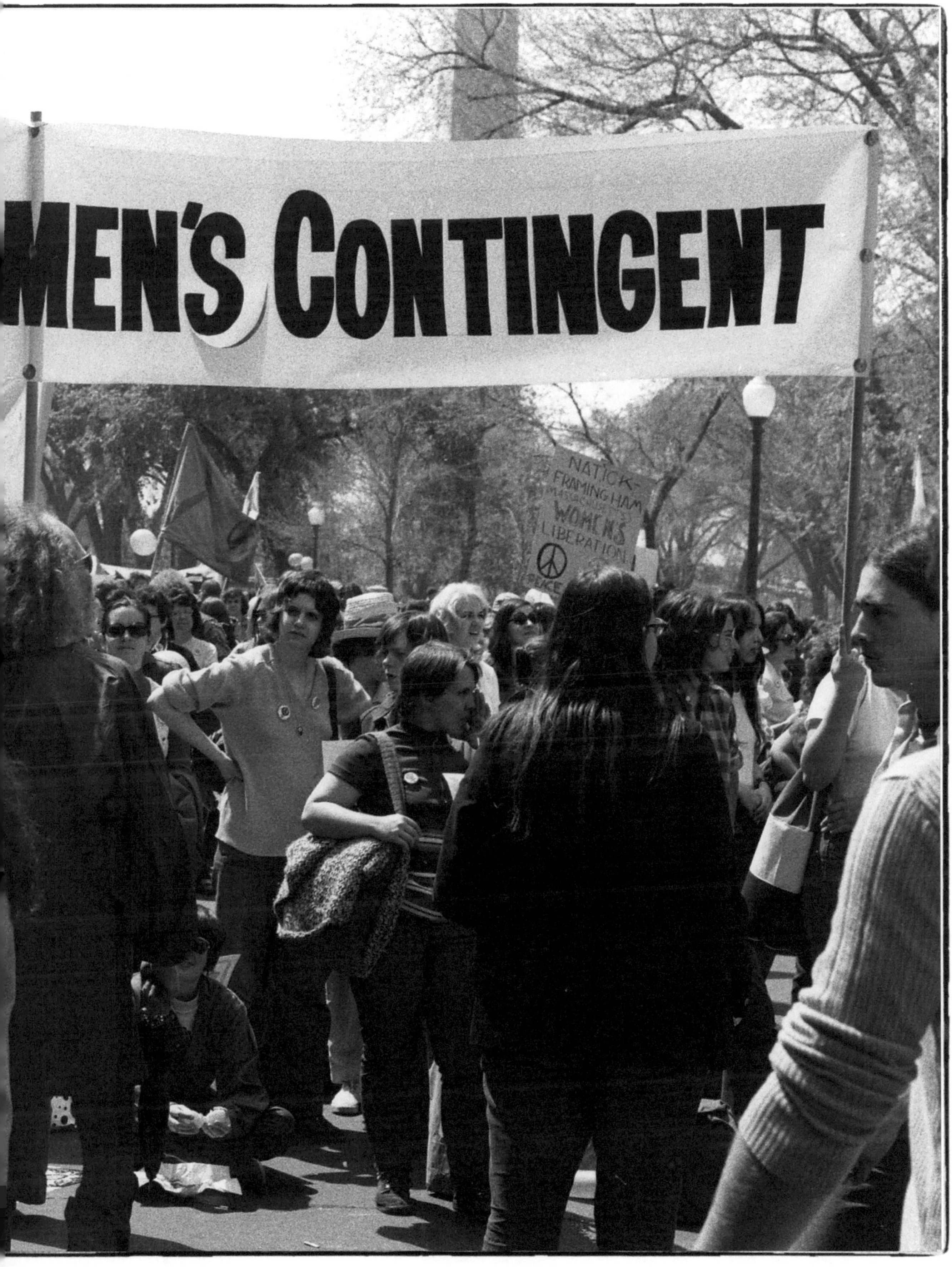
MEN'S CONTINGENT
NATICK-
FRAMINGHAM
WOMEN'S
LIBERATION

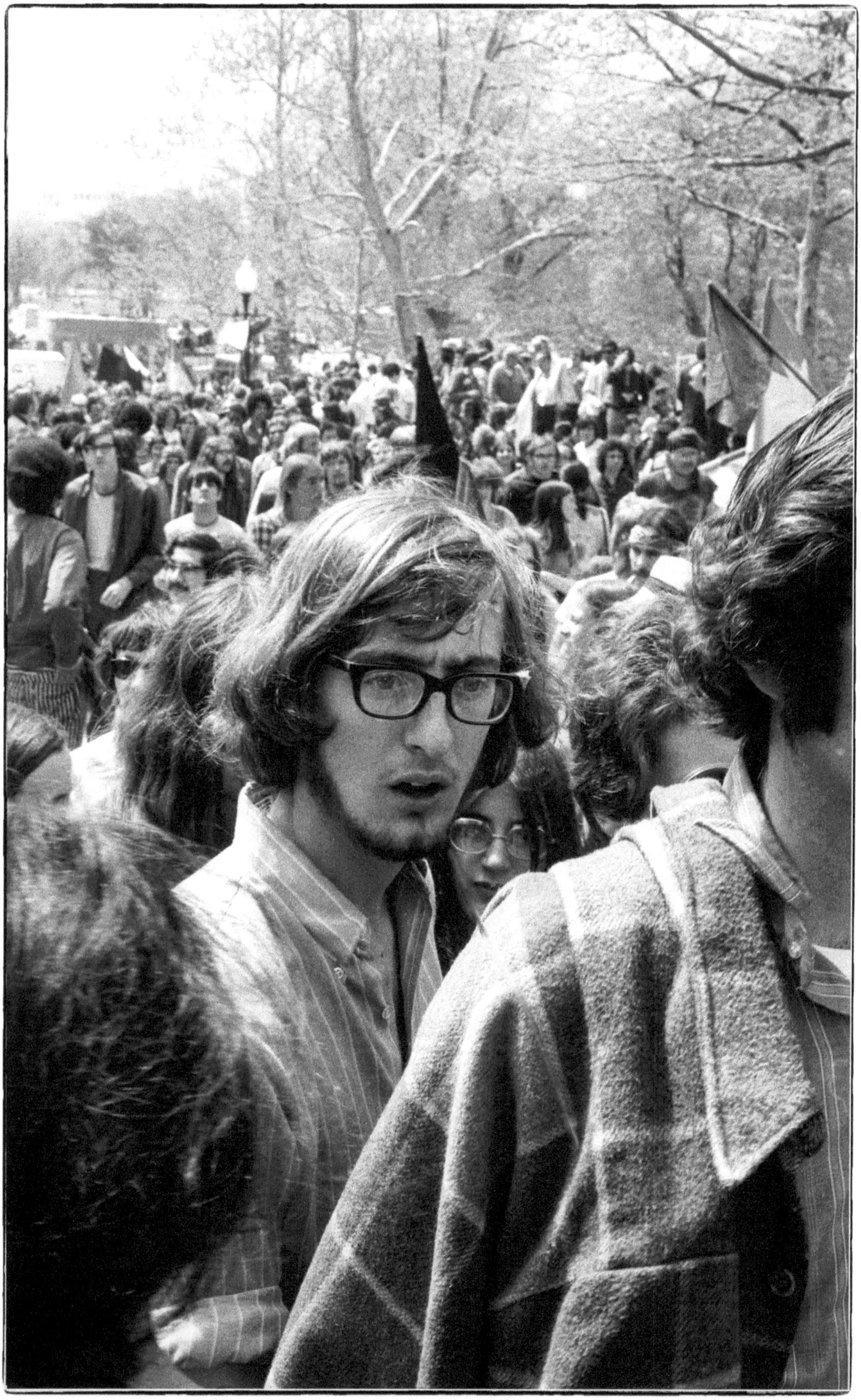

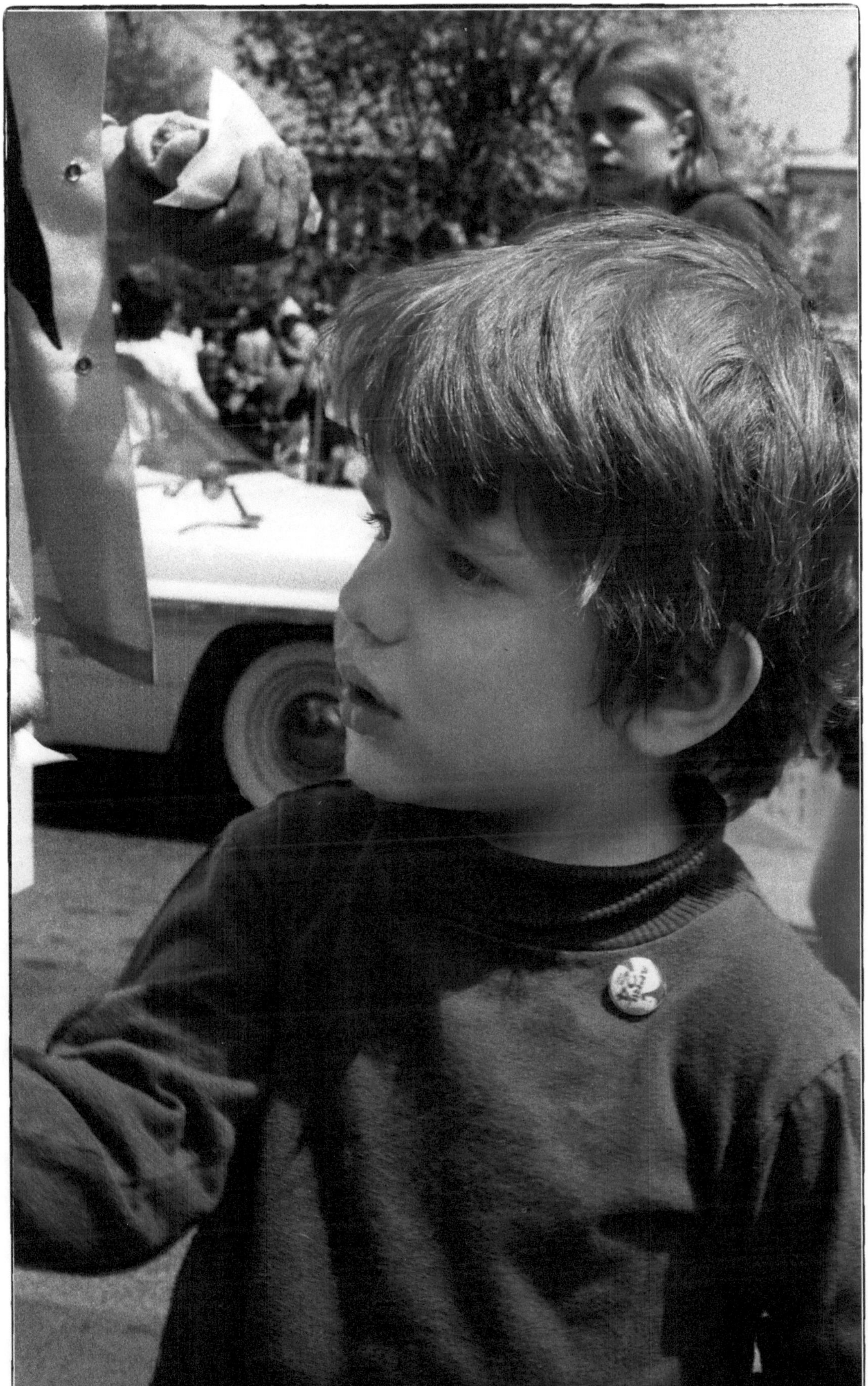

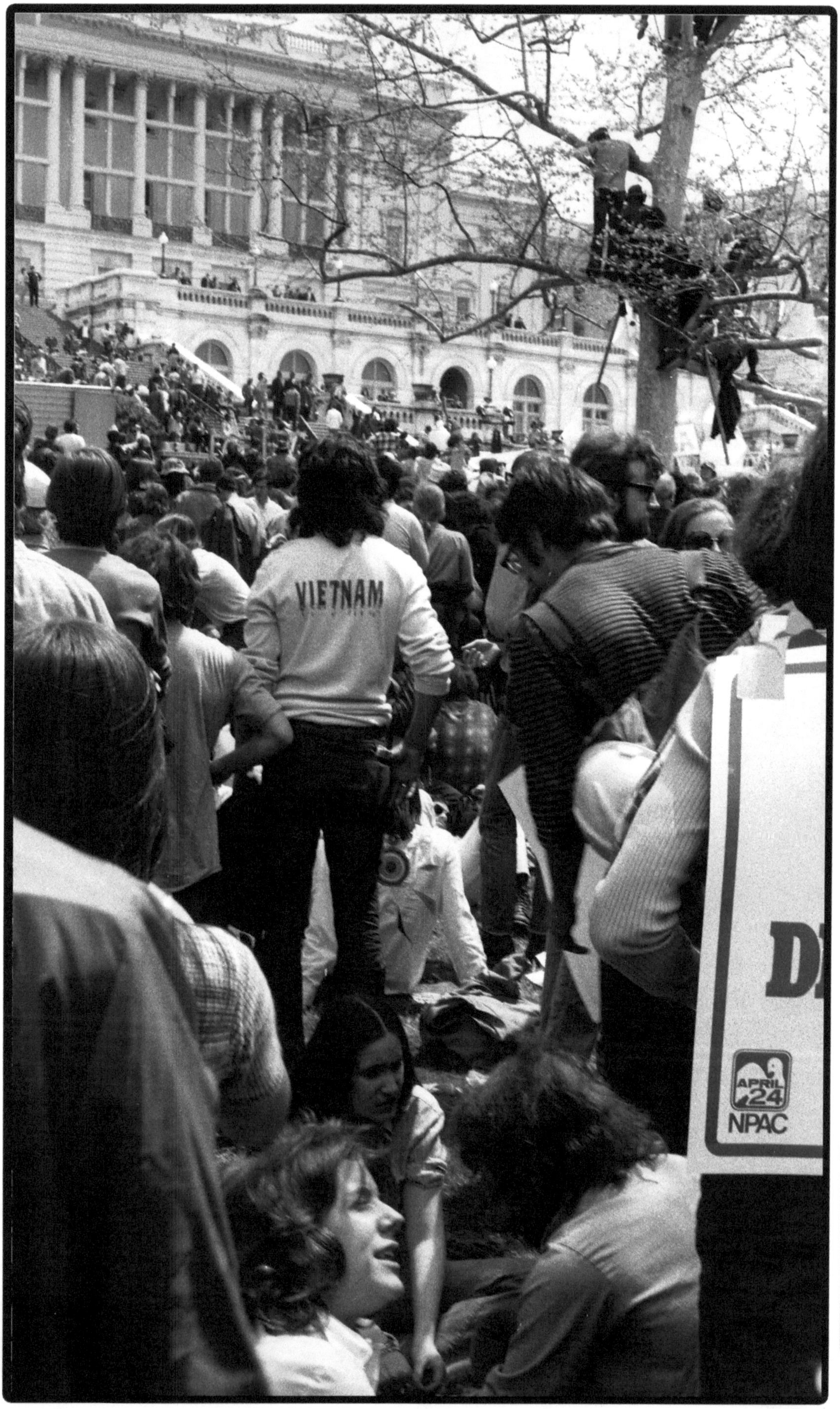
VIETNAM
APRIL 24
NPAC

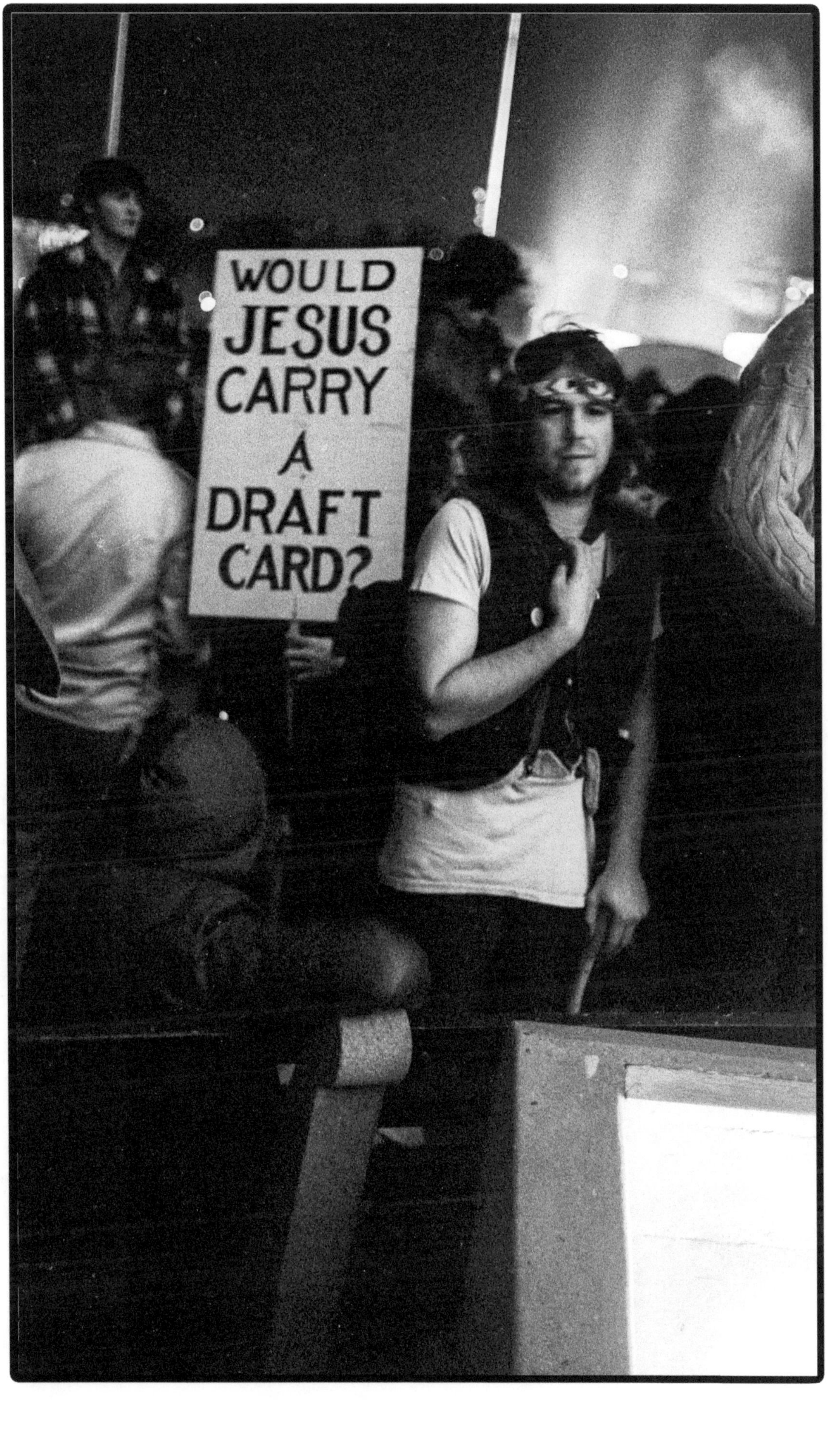
WOULD
JESUS
CARRY
A
DRAFT
CARD?

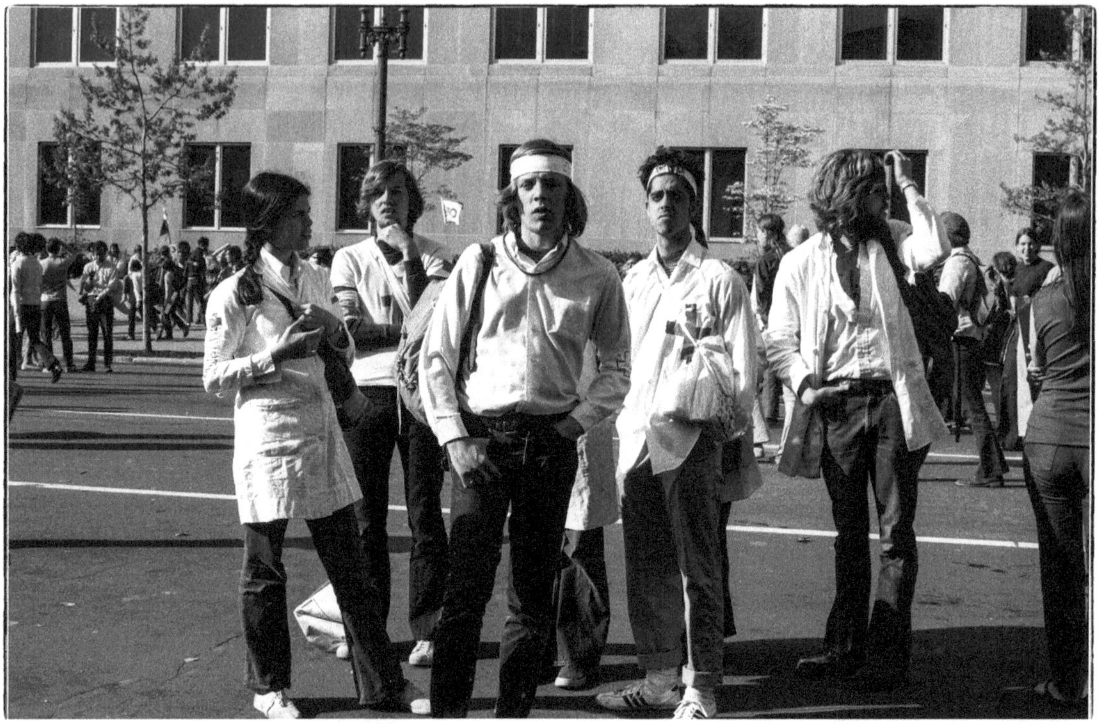

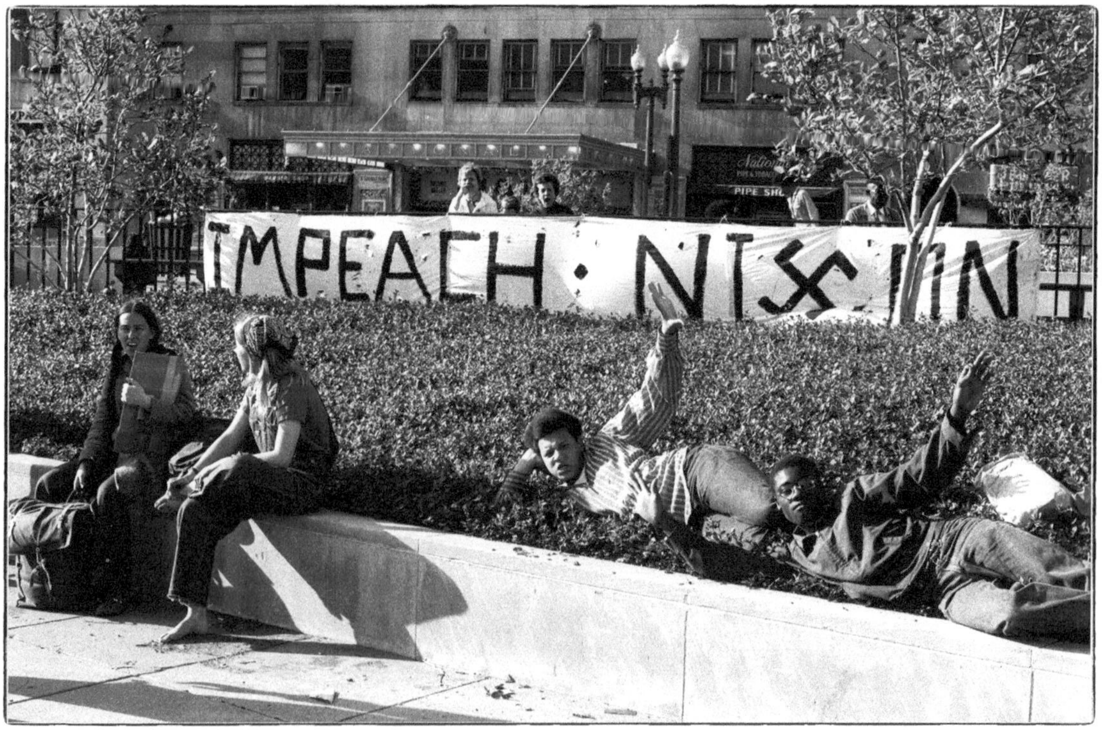
IMPEACH

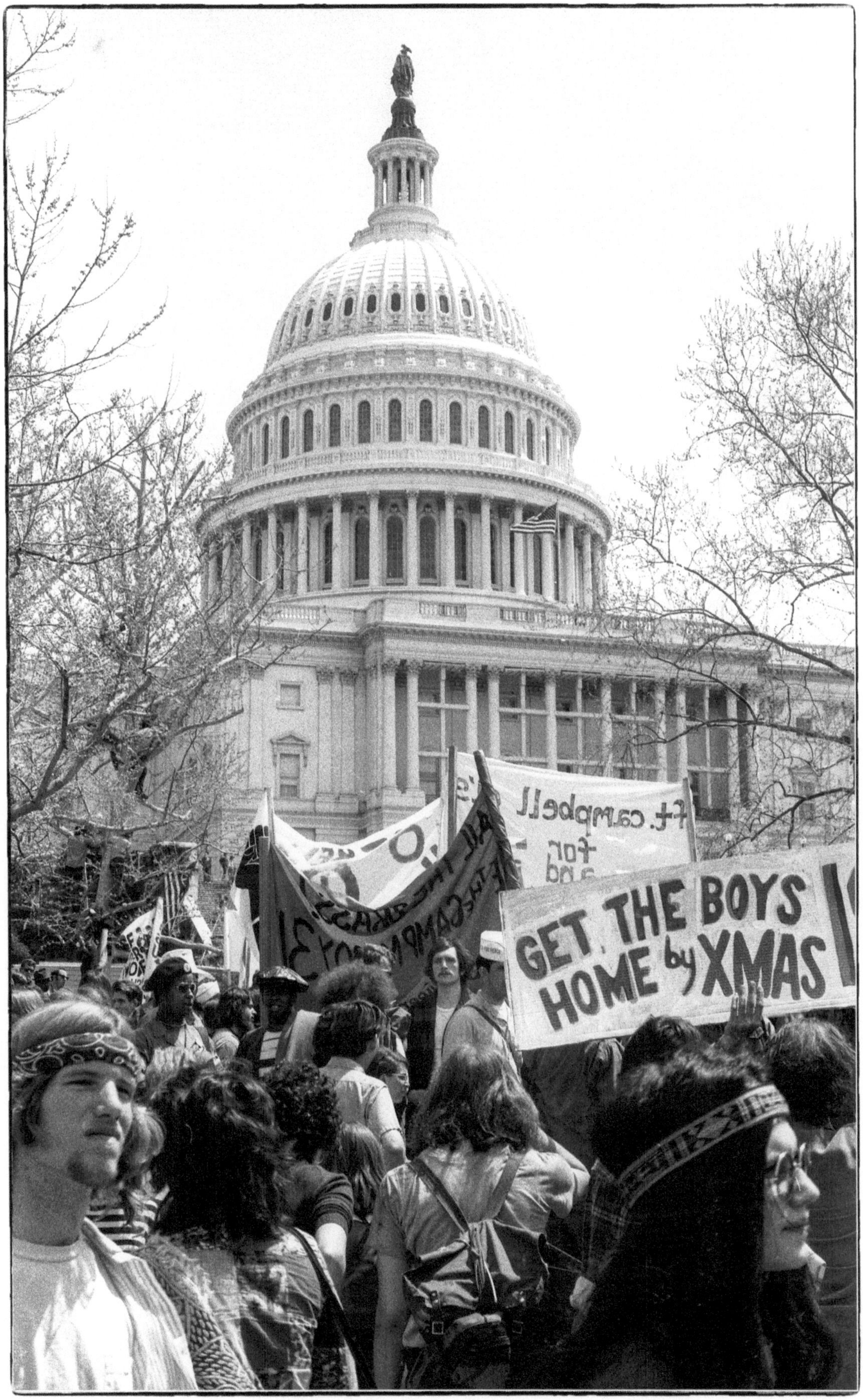
ft. campbell
for
GET THE BOYS
HOME by XMAS

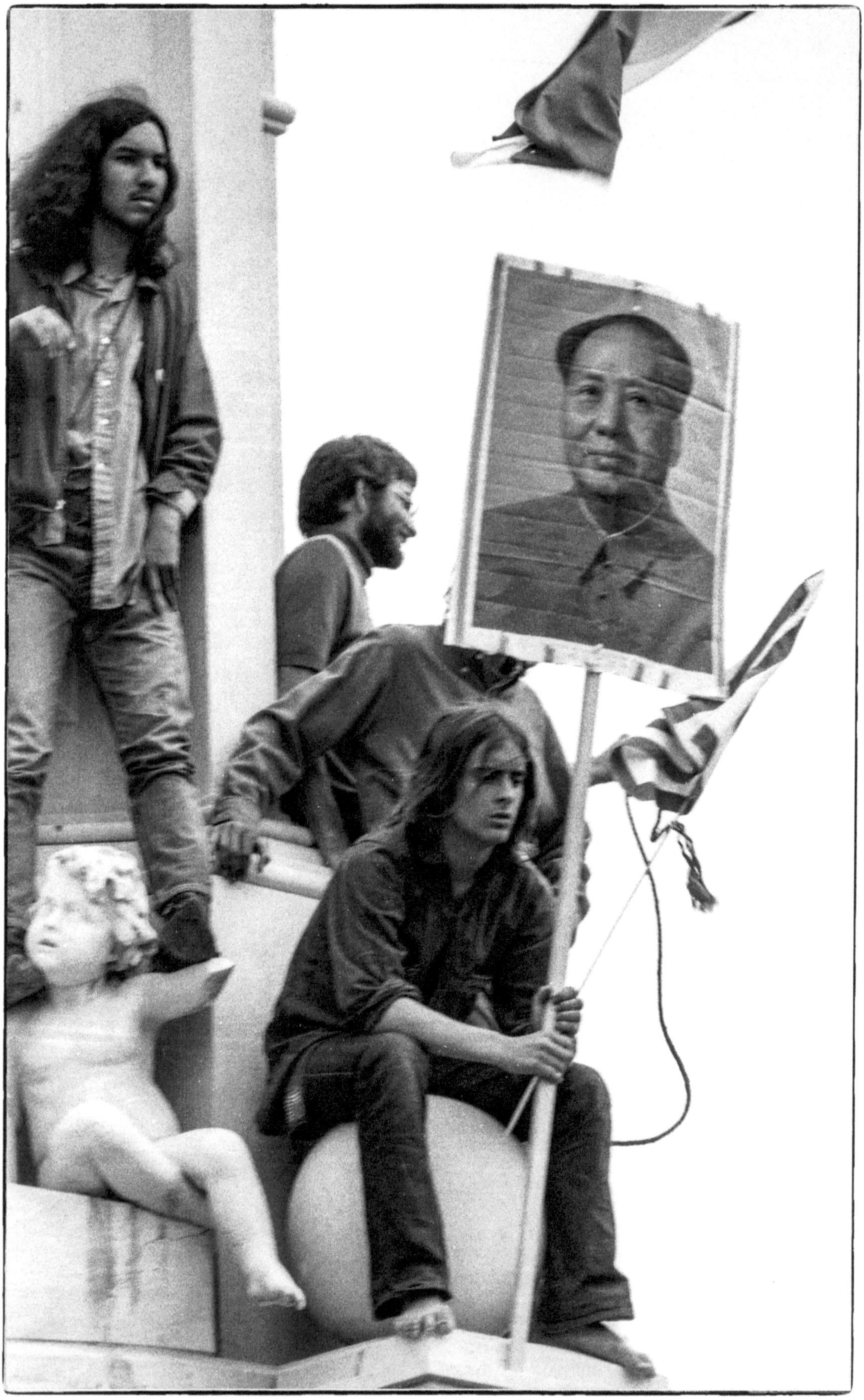

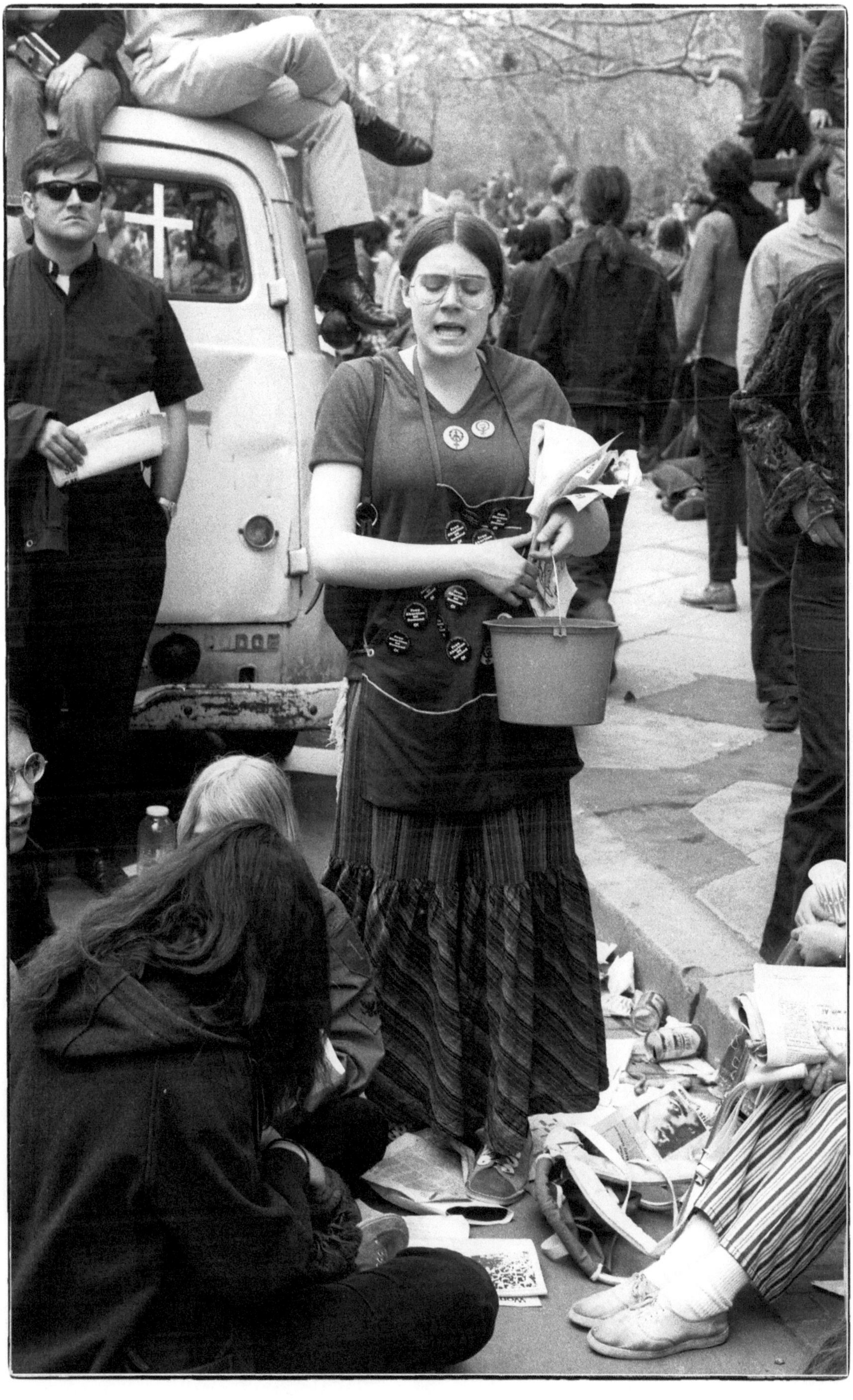

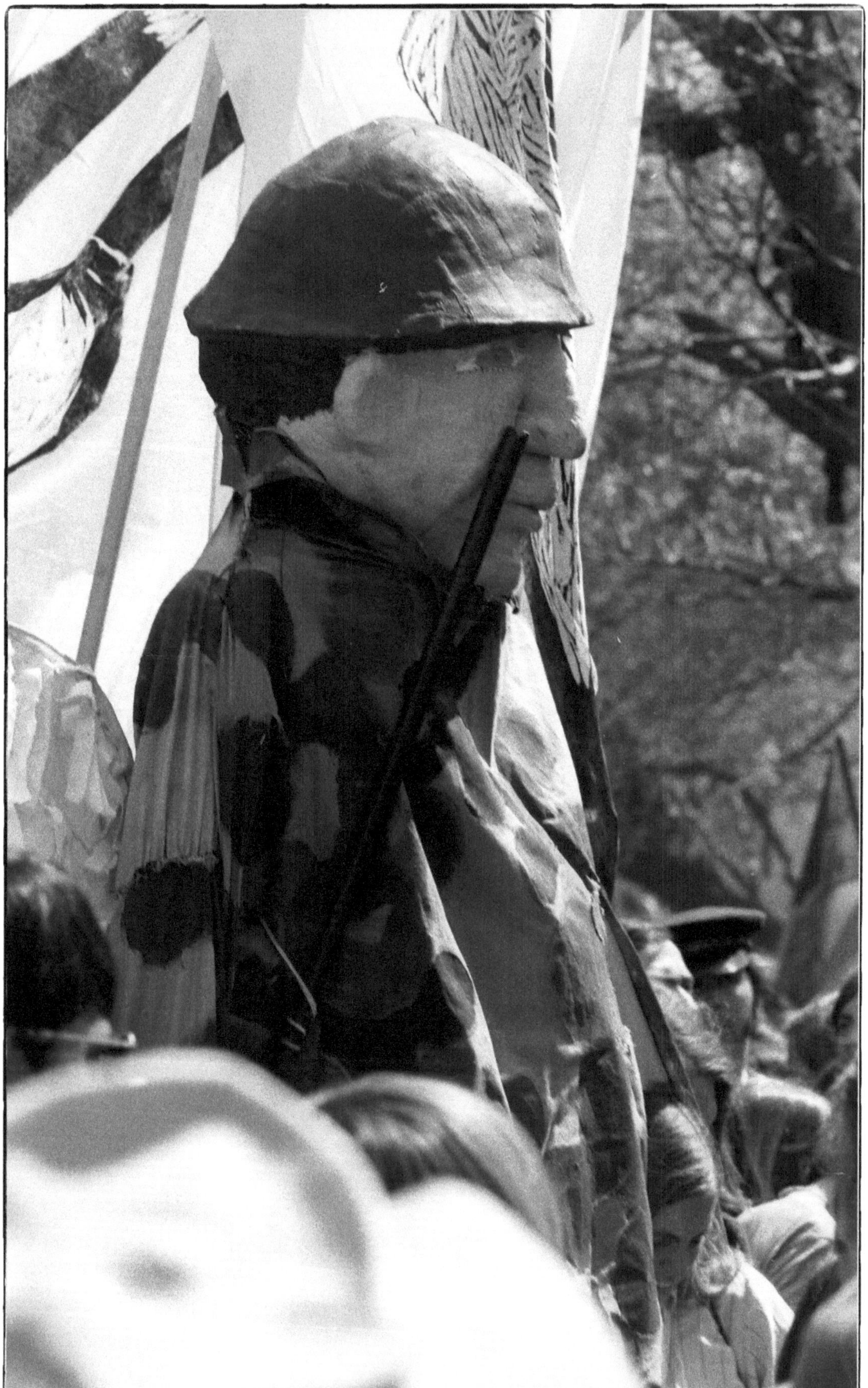

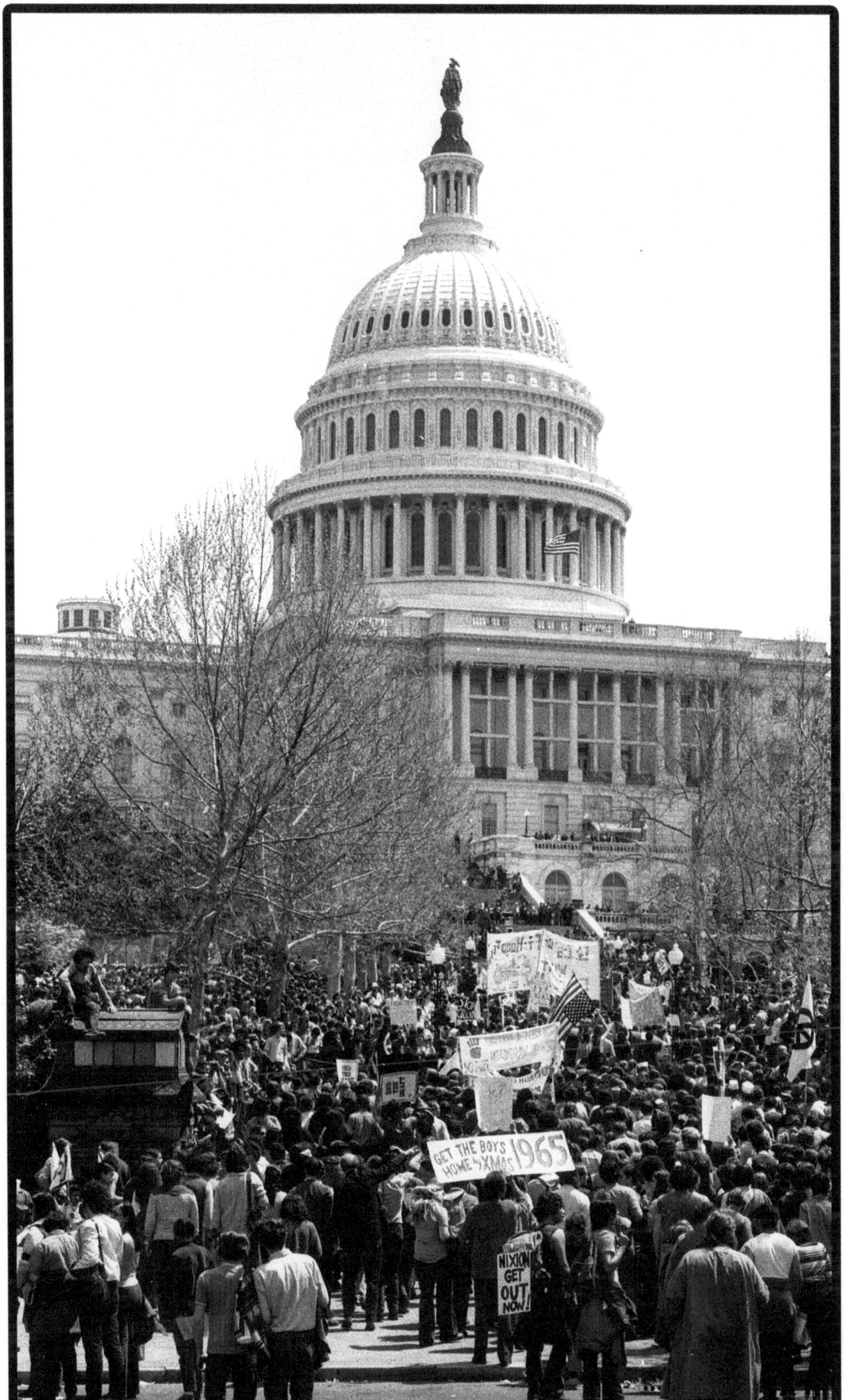
GET THE BOYS HOME by XMAS 1965
NIXION GET OUT NOW!

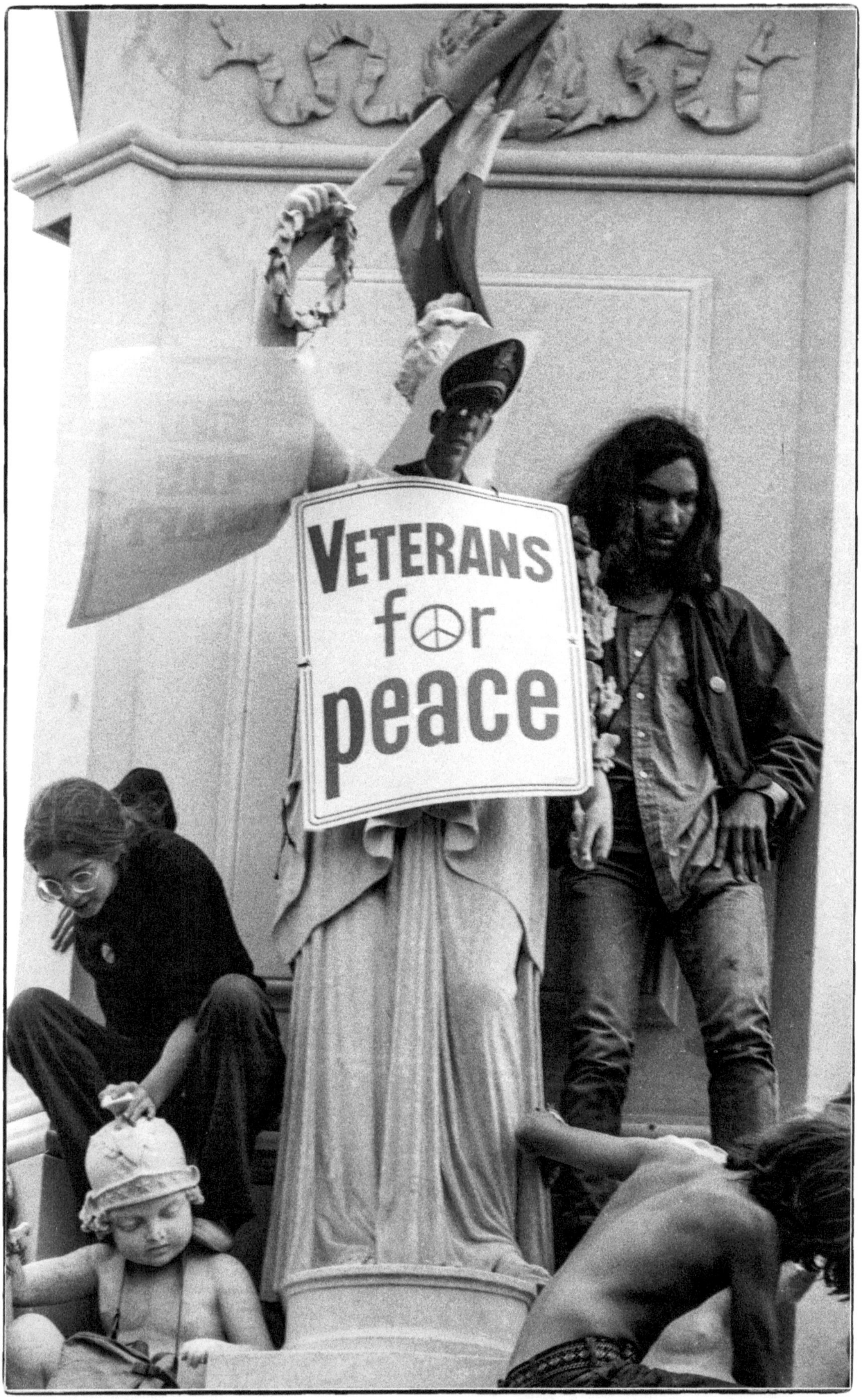
VETERANS
for
peace

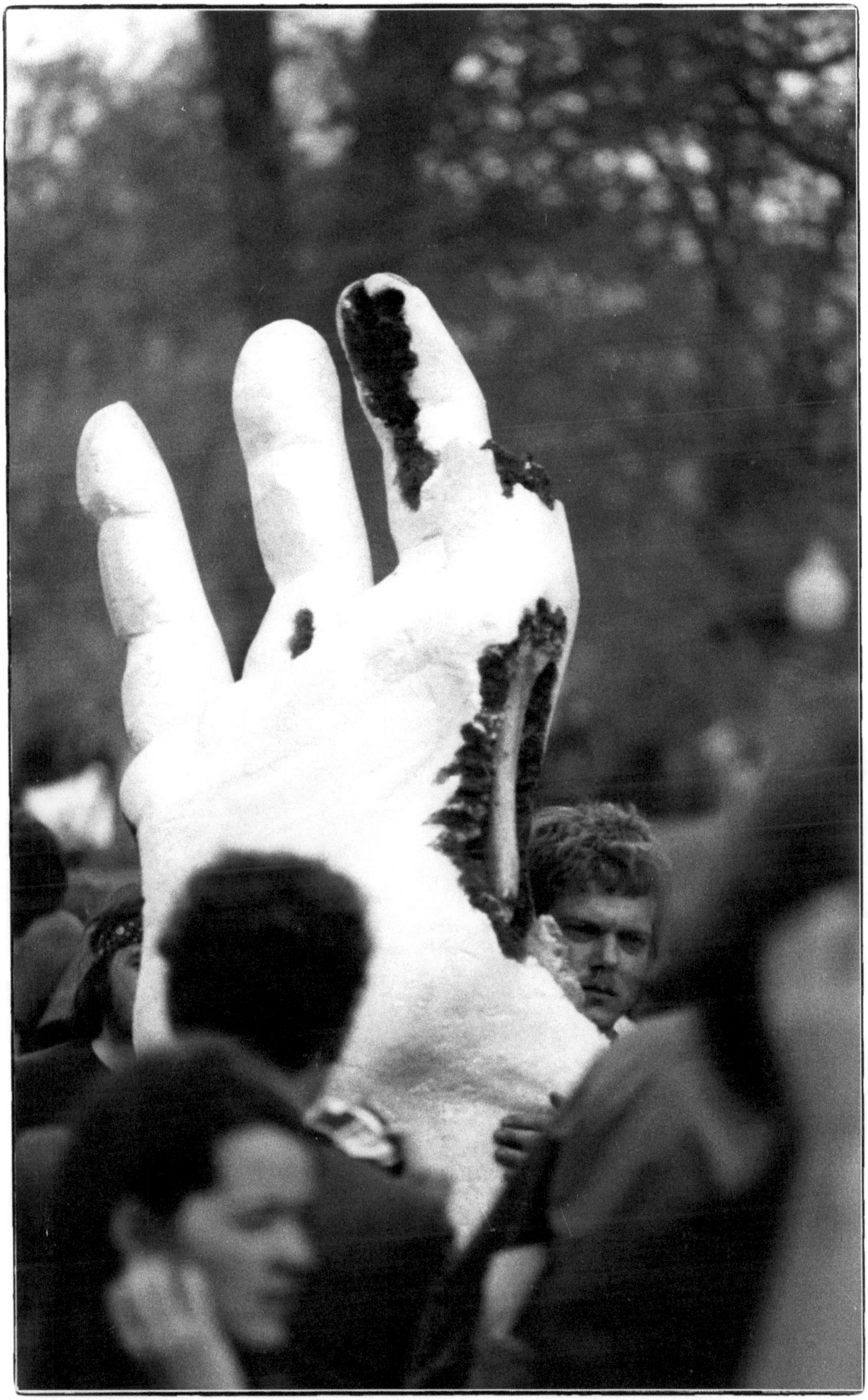

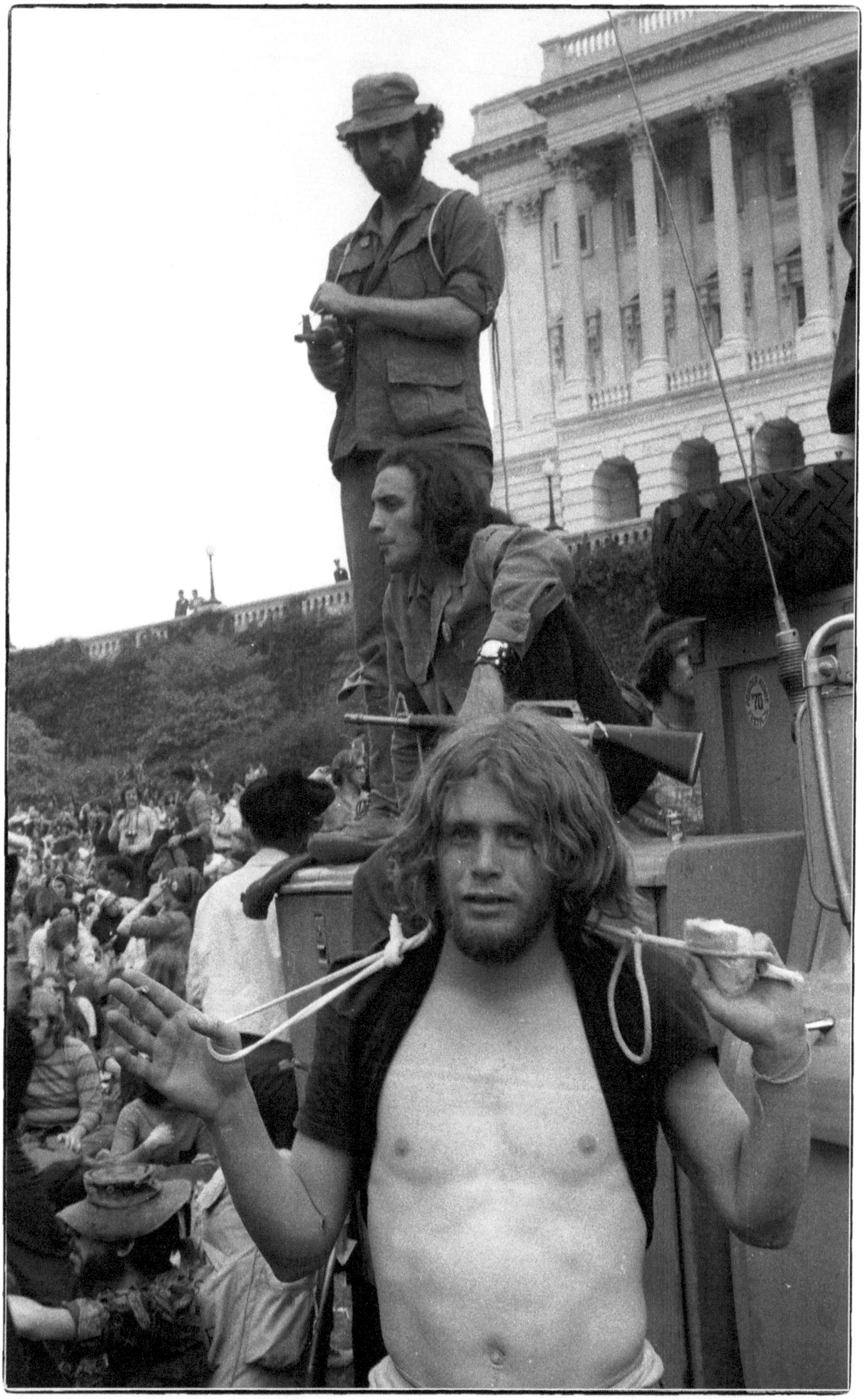

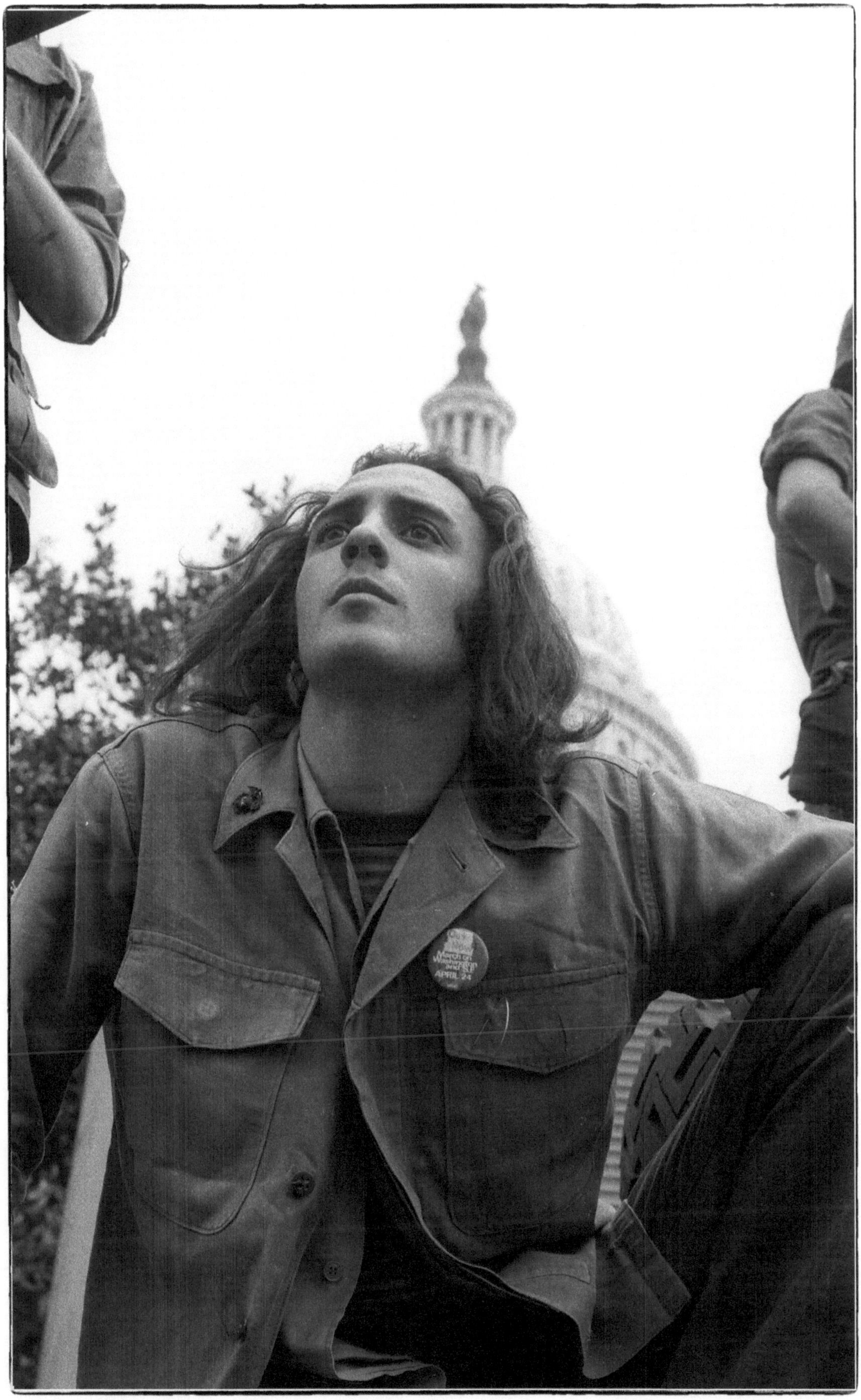
APRIL 24

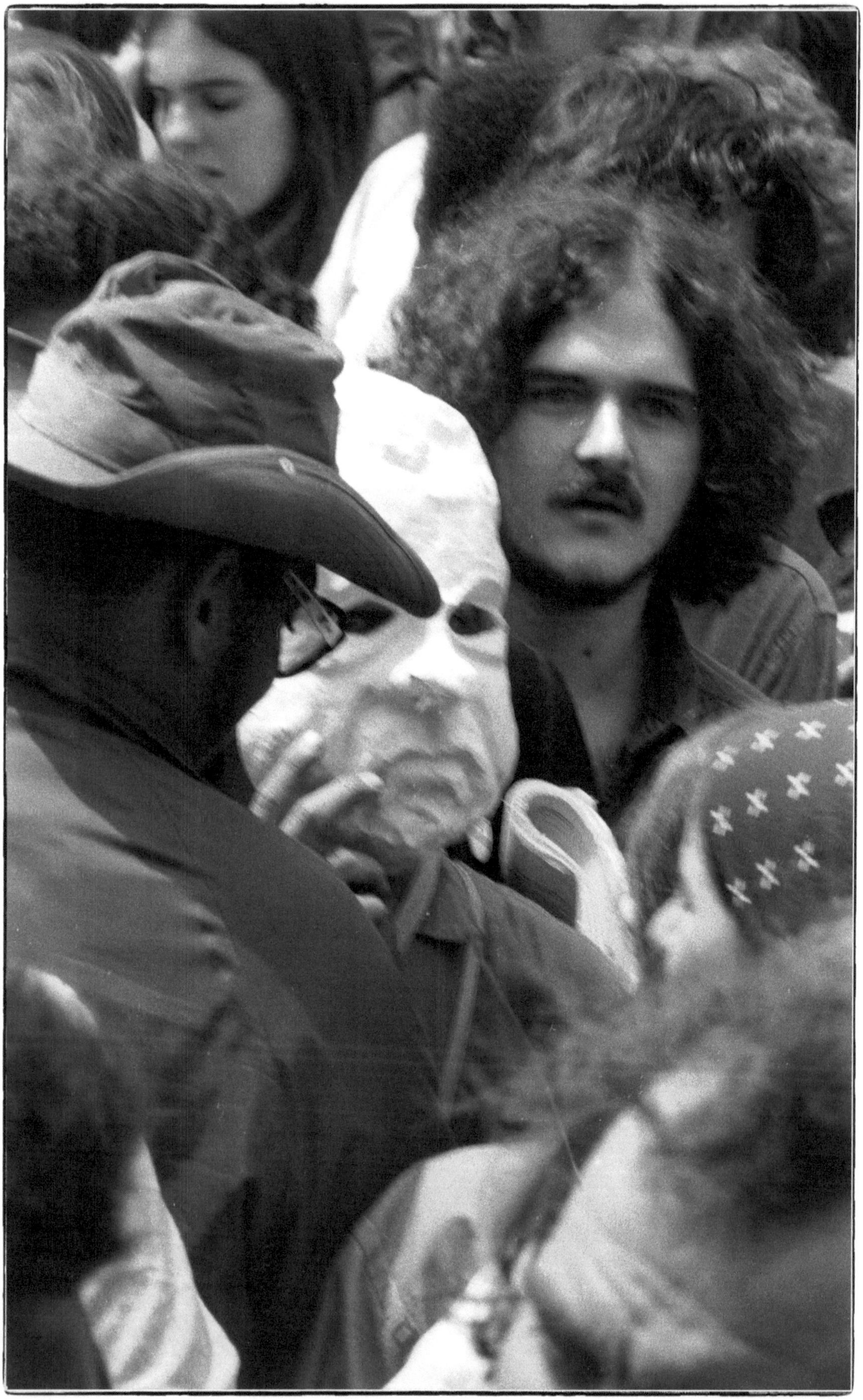

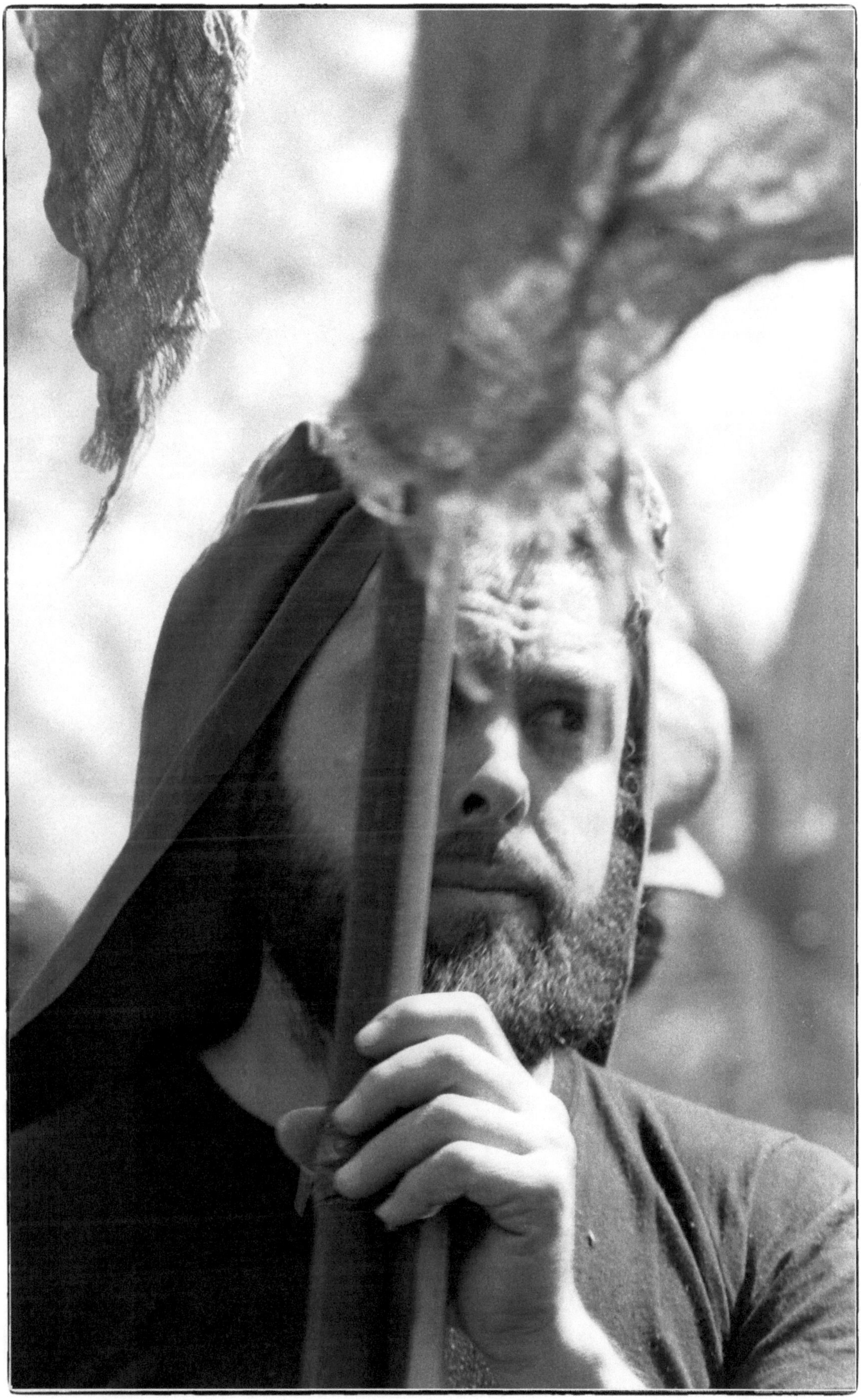

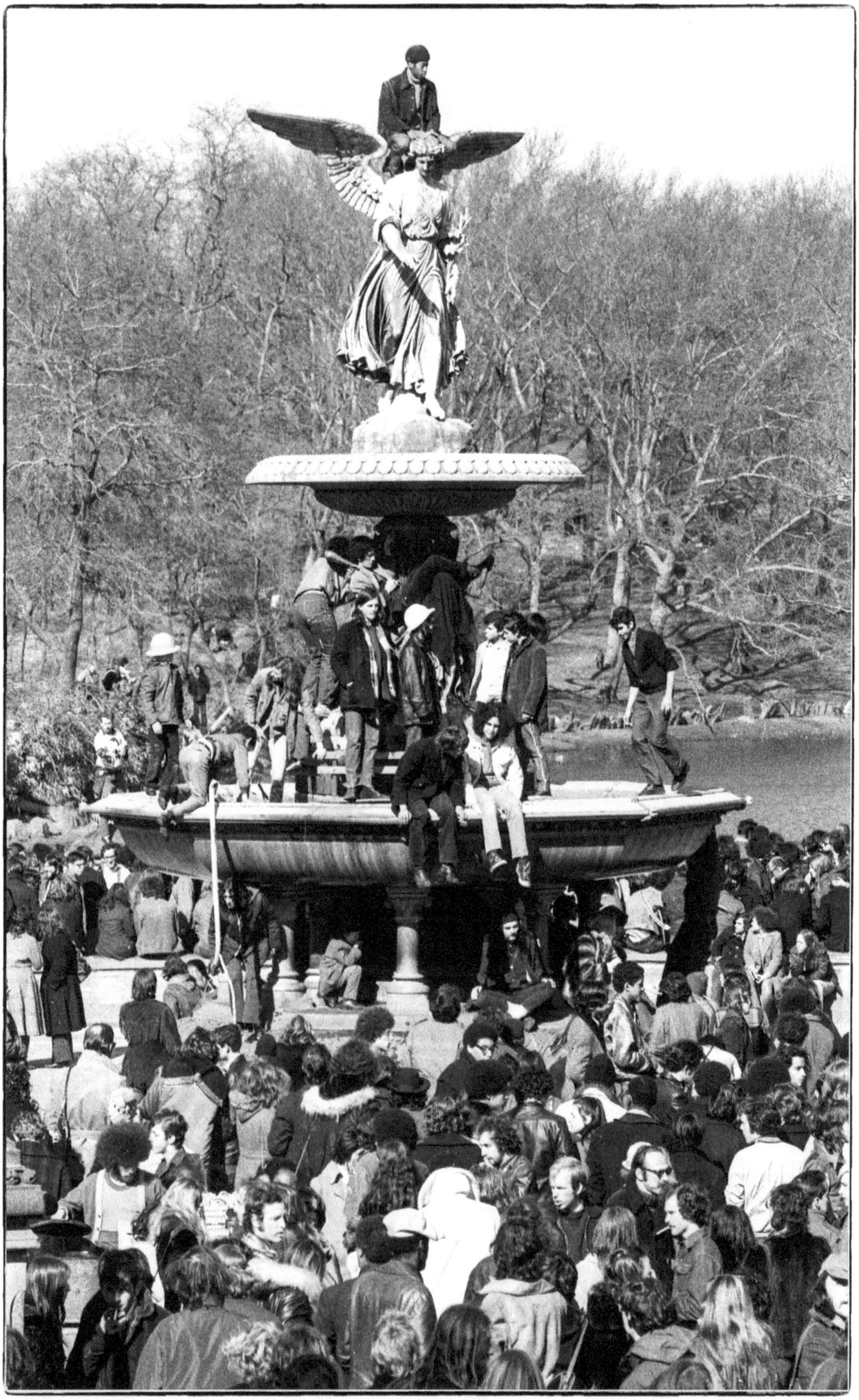

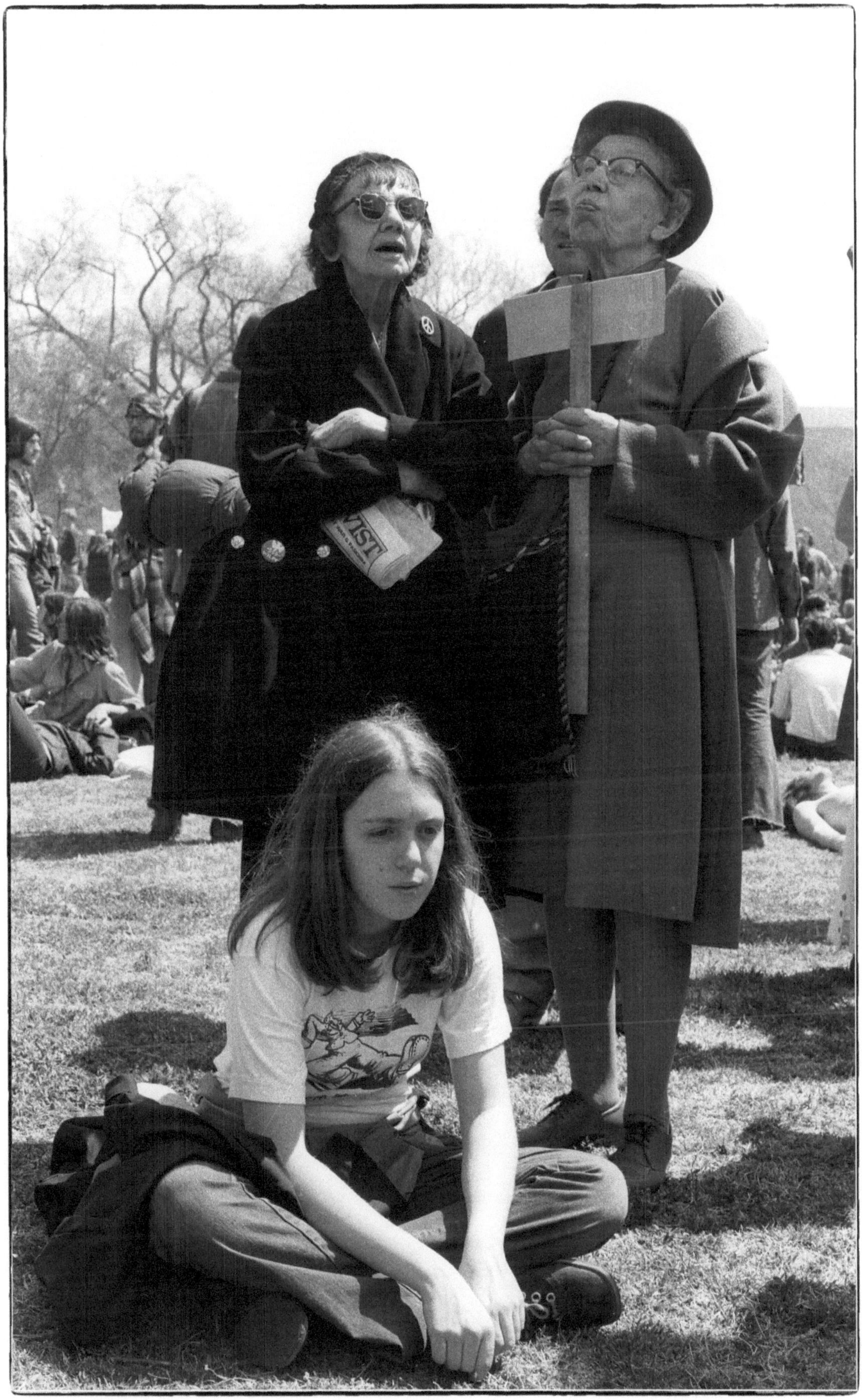

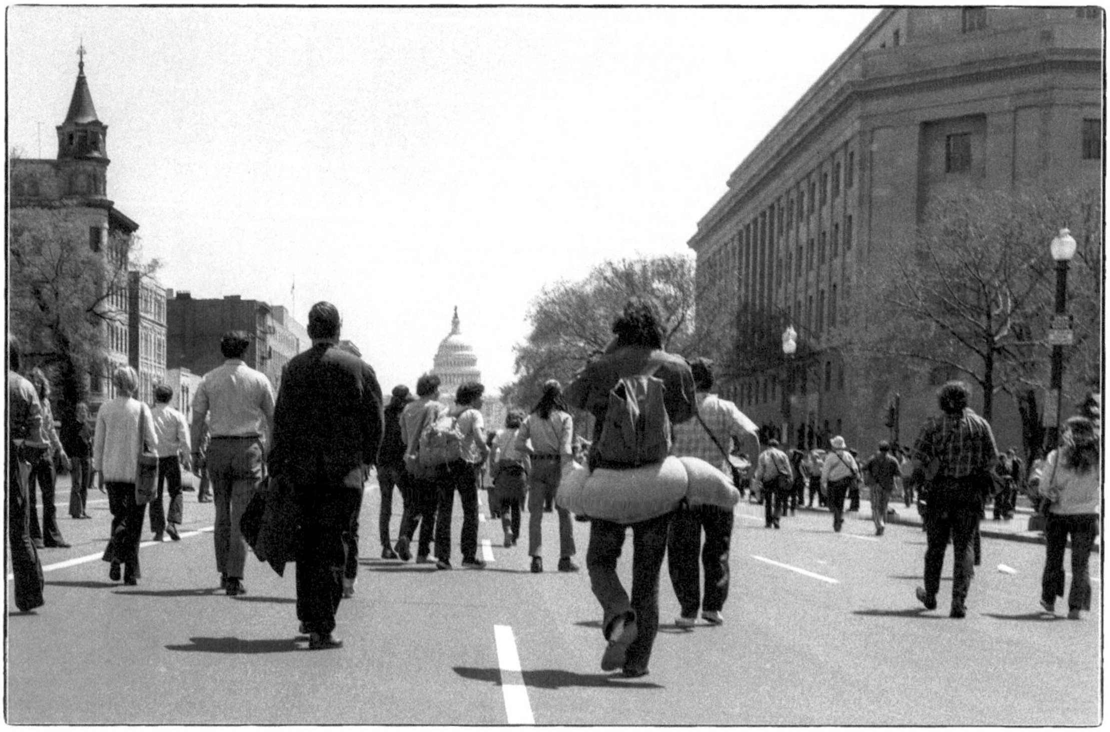

www.ingramcontent.com/pod-product-compliance
Lightning Source LLC
Chambersburg PA
CBHW051109180526
45172CB00002B/834
* 9 7 8 1 5 4 6 4 1 8 4 0 5 *